Participatory Democracy Or Descent Into Oligarchy

MR. RONALD D. SCHENCK JD

Copyright © 2012 Mr. Ronald D. Schenck JD
All rights reserved.

ISBN: 1475159412
ISBN 13: 9781475159417

CONTENTS

Preface	v
Chapter One *Freedom In Our Democracy*	1
Chapter Two *Religious Freedom*	11
Chapter Three *Constitutional Participatory Government*	21
Chapter Four *The Constitution And The Death Penalty*	29
Chapter Five *Judges*	39
Chapter Six *The Two Party System*	45
Chapter Seven *Education And The Public Schools*	59
Chapter Eight *Immigration In 2012*	67
Chapter Nine *Foreign Policy & International Relations*	73
Chapter Ten *The Right To Bear Arms*	83
Chapter Eleven *The Current Political Scene*	91
Chapter Twelve *The Coming 2012 Election*	99

Chapter Thirteen
   The Occupy Movement   *105*
Post Script   109
Case Law Citations   113
INDEX-citations to statistical research and law   115

PREFACE

CONSTITUTIONAL PARTICIPATORY GOVERNMENT

The main theme of this book is a plea for a return to significant citizen participation in all levels and branches of government.
This requires:

1) Term limits at all levels and branches of government;
2) A societal framework which gives and or leaves citizens with time, energy and sufficient financial security to participate in community and government and still meet the duties and needs of personal and family life.
3) We must re-tool, re-tune and modernize our democratic political system to meet the challenges of the 21st Century. The Two Party system must go. A strong third party must be formed.
4) Reversal of Citizens United v. Fed. Election Comm. Only human citizens -people-, individually or in groups of one mind , should be permitted to speak freely in the political/government arena.

If we do not achieve a return to large majority participation in politics and government our democracy is doomed. Class warfare will increase. The wealthy few and their political prostitutes will rule – leading to Oligarchy!
Where are the good, decent men and women (not perfect) who are not married to the ultra liberal left wing or the ultra conservative right wing? Men and women who realize that democratic government is not my way or the highway, but a deliberative process, where compromise is not a dirty word. Democracy is not a two-party system. It is a system that should encourage the participation of all human citizens in political discourse.

Participatory Democracy Or Descent Into Oligarchy

Democracy is a participatory, regenerative process or it fails to meet its promise of freedom and opportunity for all and chokes on its stagnation.

Class, (as in upper class, middle class, lower class) should not exist in a permanent or semipermanent way or be defined in terms of wealth, social status or power – political, religious, or other.

Wealth, at least in terms of a large percent of a democracy's wealth, should not roll over from generation to generation of the same families by inheritance.

We need to retool, re-tune and bring our government structure out of the 18th century and into the 21st century to enable it to meet our modern economic and social problems and to protect our fundamental freedoms.

Where are the moderate, secure, educated, decent (not perfect) tolerant citizens who:

1) place freedom first, for all human beings;
2) do not need or expect government to support or advance their religious faith or lack of it;
3) understand and support the First Amendment guarantee to every citizen freedom of and from religion, specifically, freedom from a government adopted and supported religious faith and freedom of every citizen to have no religious faith.
4) are secure enough in their own religious faith, or lack of religious faith, to respect and be tolerant of the religious faith or lack thereof of others.
5) do not feel the need to judge human beings who are not made from the standard mold, e g homosexuals, and to fear and hate them!

Oligarchy

(From Greek-oligos- meaning a few-; archo-meaning to rule, govern, command)

Oligarchy is a form of government in which power effectively rests with a small number of people. These people can be distinguished by wealth, family ties, corporate or military control, who pass their power from one generation to the next.

DEDICATION

THIS BOOK IS DEDICATED TO THE MEMORY OF MY FOREFATHERS WHO FROM THE TIME OF LANDING IN AMERICA HAVE WORKED AND FOUGHT FOR FREEDOM AND TO MY SEVEN BROTHERS WHO SERVED IN THE ARMED FORCES IN WW 2 DEFENDING FREEDOM.

Chapter One

FREEDOM IN OUR DEMOCRACY

The Constitution of the United States of America guarantees to the " people":

I. Freedom:

    A. Of and from religion;
    B. Of speech
    C. Of the press;
    D. Of assembly and association;
    E. To petition the government;
    F. To bear arms

II. Freedom From:

    A. unreasonable searches and seizures of persons, homes, papers, Etc.

- B. Warrants issued without probable cause and not supported by oath describing in particular the place to be searched or the person or persons and/or things to be seized;
- C. being placed in double jeopardy – being charged and tried twice for the same crime;
- D. self-incrimination – being a witness against one's self;
- E. government taking property from citizens for other than public use and or without just compensation:

III. Certain Personal Rights

- A. Freedom to assemble and or associate for any lawful purpose or cause and/or any purpose or cause which does not deny to other citizens freedoms guaranteed to all citizens and do not involve treason or the promotion of treason;
- B. To be free from criminal prosecution without due process of law;
- C. to be free from being deprived of life, liberty or property without due process of law;
- D. To be free from being held to answer for a capital crime or other infamous crime unless indicted for such by a grand jury;
- E. to a speedy public trial by an impartial jury chosen from the state or district where the crime is alleged to have been committed;
- F. to be confronted by the witnesses against you;
- G. to have use of the justice system to compel witnesses in the accused's favor to appear and testify;
- H. to have assistance of counsel in the defense of a criminal charge or charges;
- I. to trial by jury in civil cases (involving claims above a certain monetary amount);
- J. to a reasonable bail to assure appearance;
- K. to not be subject to or required to pay excessive fines;
- L. to not be subjected to cruel and unusual punishment;
- M. to be free from discrimination by government or entities, or citizens based on sex, race, color, creed or ethnic origin.

Mr. Ronald D. Schenck JD

The protections of freedom provided by the Constitution are great and essential to a free society, but freedom can be and is constrained by many other factors in life:

1) population;
2) income/poverty; lack of sufficient income or wealth to provide the basic necessities of life;
3) lack of opportunity;
4) lack of education;
5) poor health;
6) environment;
7) personal beliefs ,e.g. religious;

In the world we now live in, population obviously has the greatest impact on our personal freedoms. Population can and does exacerbate many of the limiting conditions cited above.

The agrarian society that existed when the United States was formed and the vast expanse of largely unpopulated land no longer exists. Not many of us live in sufficient isolation from our nearest neighbors to avoid the health, sanitation, environmental and safety laws which everyone is subject to in our modern civilized society.

The greater in number the population becomes the more personal freedom individuals forfeit and the more responsibility each citizen has to take care not to selfishly and unnecessarily infringe on the freedom of others. Mutual individual and societal responsibility has grown exponentially with a growing population.

The past century has seen an increasingly rapid growth of population in the United States and worldwide.

The Great Depression of the 1930s drove home our ever increasing mutual social responsibility – to create a societal structure that would, to at least a minimum level, provide basic living necessities for even the weakest, less gifted of us: e.g. food, shelter, health care, clothing, education and transportation.

We would no longer permit the widespread hunger and homeless existence of citizens living in poverty for reasons mostly or entirely out of their control, including those unable to compete in an increasingly complex society.

It now is apparent that these lessons have faded into history (or are intentionally ignored by a significant segment of our citizenry). There is a powerful movement to abolish or at least sharply reduce the societal safety net programs put in place since the Great Depression.

The growth of our population, resulting in similar growth in the number of citizens needing assistance together with additions to the government assistance provided, e.g. food stamps, and the raising of the level and quality of the assistance programs, compounded by the decline of the income and economic opportunities of our middle income citizens, has created a backlash of resistance amongst the upper middle class and the wealthy citizenry against the taxes levied to pay the cost of these programs and support the bureaucracy!!

This resistance comes mainly from the " baby boomer" generation and their offspring who have never experienced a Great Depression and the resulting abject poverty and hopelessness of millions of citizens, the cause of which they had no hand in. You see a lot of the " baby boomers" in the tea party!

The recent Occupy movement participants, mostly from the college-age and younger citizens, seem to have caught on to the fact that their opportunities to get an education and be able to earn an income sufficient to provide a lifestyle similar to that which their parents and grandparents have enjoyed is seriously threatened by the economic policies being pushed by " the have's". They call them the 1%.

Freedom and democracy does not include the right to amass and control a major portion of the economic assets and, therefore, the power to control the distribution of wealth, the political process and who pays the cost of government.

The assertion by those now holding a large portion of the economic power that our nation was built by capitalism/free enterprise and, therefore, capitalism and free enterprise are the foundations of our free democracy and, therefore, in effect constitutionally protected rights is a big lie!

Capitalism, taken to its extreme, can be and is as destructive of freedom and democratic government as are communism, socialism, monarchies and any other forms of government which own and or control the assets of a nation and its citizens.

If 1% of the population, or 25%,owns or controls 90% or more of the assets, capital of a nation, and that ownership is rolled over from generation to generation and these wealthy few control the government, then the government in effect controls the nation's assets – " capital".

If they figure out, as the George W. Bush administration did, how to control a major part of the electorate by using religion, fear, racism, ignorance etc., then they also can control the government. That equals Oligarchy! In this day and age, mind control is becoming more and more a science rather than an art!

Religion has been the main tool used by despotic governments, e.g. monarchies, over millenniums to control the masses! The threat of hell and the promise of heaven and eternal life still works!

More mundane threats to our freedom have risen from actions and inaction by our government due mainly to the control of government by the two-party system. One glaring area is permitting the rapid growth of dependence on foreign oil, even after the clear wake-up call in the early '70s when the Middle East producers cut off our supply. This dependence not only threatens but has reduced our freedom, personal and as a nation. We have continued to build vehicles and industrial and public infrastructure which require an ever increasing supply of oil and gas Whether you drive an 8 mile per gallon vehicle or a 50 mile per gallon vehicle, you're able to get to where you want to go. Your basic freedom is not constricted. Large population centers need mass transit instead of 10 lane wide freeways. The development of alternate energy sources, happening now, has not been a priority. The bottom line has been and is the priority!

Freedom is a relative concept. Freedom means that a citizen can carry out his or her life with the least possible need to adjust his or her actions and needs to accommodate and not degrade unnecessarily the freedom of other citizens. It does not mean that the definition of freedom is to succeed in business. or make millions ,or inherit millions/ billions.. The American dream is not defined so narrowly and selfishly. Neither is freedom defined by capitalism or free enterprise!!

Freedom-Not So Simple

Life without freedom is slavery, no matter how enforced or controlled, and slavery is a crime.

To maintain maximum freedom for all citizens requires a Democratic government which maintains a balance of power of all kinds amongst its citizens. Freedom in a democracy is not just the right or property of the privileged, or of the wealthy or of those blessed with talents, or good luck or inheritance.

Each newborn citizen of the United States should have an equal shot, relative to their abilities and the productive use of their abilities, to at least a fair share of the country's wealth in order to enjoy maximum freedom and to live a free, secure and rewarding life.

In our recent history we have, on a rather steep curve, devalued the contributions of a large portion of our population (the "middle and a lower income class") and increased exponentially the value of the contributions of a small portion of our population e.g., the capitalist's, CEO's, and the wealthy.

Our democracy will not survive this trend. Sooner or later democracy will collapse with the weight of keeping the privileged few. Trickle-down economics does not work and has never worked to justly compensate the contributions of the complex and widely varying talents of our citizens to our economy and social infrastructure.

True Democratic government (not the Democratic Party) must use it's power to provide an economic and social structure that, as fairly as reasonably possible, distributes the national wealth as equitably as possible.

This does not call for government ownership of the nations economic structure or assets of any kind. (E. G. Socialism). The government regulated system of free enterprise which has been fundamental to our economy and way of life since before our independence would go on without a capitalist/ free enterprise economy that permits the privileged few to control all or a major portion of the nations assets. Freedom in a democracy requires a fair system of taxation and fair compensation, from bottom to top, for contributions to the economy and social structure together with a legal system which fairly regulates personal and economic activity.

Our tax system is totally out of balance and totally out of control. Big, medium and small businesses have not paid their fair share of taxes to maintain and improve the infrastructure of this country which they are the major users of, especially over the last 30 to 50 years. As a result our infrastructure is in bad shape.

Inheritance and gift taxes have been a part of our tax system since the inception of our democracy. Our present Federal estate and gift tax law provides that the first 5 million of an estate not be taxed. All above 5 million is taxed at 35 %. There are many loopholes and dodges!!

Under this law, the very wealthy can leave the largest portion of their estate to their heirs who usually have had no, or very little, participation in producing it. They are also usually not the free enterprise, new business creators, of their generation. I am sure most children would be ecstatic to inherit a million dollars or a share of 5 million!! Permitting the inheritance of tens of millions or billions by a very few, in time, creates the concentration of a nations wealth in a very few.

The free enterprise new business creators of each new generation and their new business's must then pay higher income and other taxes to support the inheritances of the few. Our founders recognized this threat to freedom and democracy. The asset value of an estate above 5 million should be taxed at 100% and most loopholes closed. Family businesses can, and always have been able to, transfer wealth to children who work in the family business and contribute to the success of the business by compensating the child , in part, by transferring ownership interest in the business and thereby reducing the value of the parents estate.

Labor had been used and abused by the "capitalists" in the early 20th century. In the '40s, '50s and '60s labor gained power and abused it. Management and investors have received a disproportionate slice of the profits from business operations and labor too little in the last 30 years. This has led to a sharp decline in the earnings of the middle and lower economic class of citizens. This power struggle is unfortunately not an equal one. Capital and, therefore its power can be controlled by a very few. Labor and the middle class are not so easily organized.. We must as a nation get control of this economic roller coaster or it will destroy our democracy!

The most severe blow to the middle and lower income classes' in the last 30 years of government supported capitalist economic policy was the destruction of a major portion of the middle and lower income class's equity in their homes, and for many, the loss of their homes. As a result of the Bush administration and Republican Congress' religious pursuit of this policy, the 2007 – 2008 collapse of the financial markets and the economic free fall which followed, resulted in the worst recession since the "Great Depression". The free market was everything, regulation was reviled and the result was disastrous.

Freedom of human beings cannot be protected by any document, legal, philosophical or religious or combinations thereof. Freedom is only protected, lasting and without significant class distinction by and with the eternal, constant and perceptive attention of a committed citizenry.

Freedom is lost by a people that loses focus and whose attention is distracted by the clever manipulation of a ruthless, greed is good, powerful minority.

A significant portion of the citizenry of the United States has lost focus and are being manipulated by a politically powerful group, which is using citizens ignorance, fear, bias, prejudice and racist makeup to get them to vote against their own best interests, e.g. economic, religious freedom and personal freedom.

This manipulation has always gone on to a certain degree by all sides of the political spectrum. However with the advent of the Reagan Administration it really took hold and grew rapidly. Ronald Reagan had very little to do with it, and I believe he would reject the current ultra-right wing economic, religious evangelical and tea party arch conservative's. They give true conservatives a bad name. By the time George H. W. Bush, a good man, was elected, they were very powerful and succeeded in destroying his presidency with their no new taxes and the demand for right wing conservative, social program cuts and appointment of ultra conservative Justices to the Supreme Court. Why George H. W. Bush appointed Clarence Thomas I will never comprehend or understand. He is a disgrace to the court. Scalia is bad enough!. Then came the arrogant pseudo-intellectual, pompous, demagogue Newt Gingrich, who launched the enactment of the kill the middle-class right-wing legislative program in the 90s which he and other ultra right wingers had developed in the 80s!

The fatal blow was delivered with the passage of the Gramm-Leach act which repealed Glass- Steagall. Sen. Phil Gramm, that staunch intellectual conservative from Texas championed this bill in the name of "free enterprise" and economic growth. Why has that great state of Texas produced so many political prostitutes in recent years. I believe George W. Bush was just a pawn for this bunch of "free enterprise", religious evangelical's and neo-con foreign policy conservatives.

The Gramm act was a major contributor to the country falling into the worst economic recession/depression since the Great Depression of the 1930s.

"Regulation" of (or any part of, for any reason) the economic free enterprise system became a socialist conspiracy or worse, never mind the lessons of our history or the definition of socialism or the several mutations in Europe. But, the champions of unregulated free enterprise e.g., less taxes on big business and the wealthy and no revisions of the tax code to remove tax breaks and subsidies for big businesses, were still able to regain control of the House of Representatives in 2010 by their tactics of shifting the blame for the recession and lack of jobs to the "big spending" Obama administration.

What was once the party of Lincoln, Teddy Roosevelt, Eisenhower, Goldwater, Nixon, Ford, Reagan, Bob Dole and even George HW Bush (my party) has been hijacked by the ultra-right wing religious evangelicals, tea party, free enterprise, no regulation, no new taxes, ultra-right-wing conservative political prostitutes.

Their system is simple, win at all costs, use any tactic, appeal to every fear, prejudice, bigotry, ignorance, and other to win. For example, fear of homosexuals, loss of religious freedom, (e.g. your child cannot pray in school!!) Muslims, terrorists.

This tactic really caught fire under Gingrich but was not going at full bore until the 2004 election when Karl Rove ran George W. Bush's re-election campaign. He made it a political art form using win at any cost tactics and every despicable method and fear tactic known to man!!!

It appears to me the main problem is that the proponents of these tactics, i.e. tea party members and others are Baby Boomers and their children. They have no concept of history, religious freedom or the evils of unregulated free enterprise.

Karl Rove will go down in history as a person of non-existent ethical standards. He and Dick Cheney made a draconian pair. Did George W. Bush with his conservative religious beliefs ever understand? His ego was big enough to accept the results, though, and to never accept some responsibility for the nation's descent into disastrous foreign wars and economic catastrophe! Not to mention the lives lost and bodies broken.

George W. Bush's administration dealt a blow to our freedom from which recovery is not at all certain. This is especially true when, in the current (2012) election cycle, you have a continuing and accelerating unholy marriage forming between ultra-conservative right wing Catholics (Santorum supporters) and ultra-right wing Protestant evangelicals, mixed with the tea party and the ultra conservative "free enterprise" economic faction!!

THE TWO PARTY SYSTEM HAS BECOME THE MOST SERIOUS THREAT TO OUR DEMOCRACY AND MUST BE ELIMINATED IF OUR DEMOCRACY AND THE FREEDOM OF ALL CITIZENS IS GOING TO SURVIVE.

Chapter Two

RELIGIOUS FREEDOM.
THE CONSTITUTION PROVIDES:

First Amendment:
 "Congress shall make no laws respecting an establishment of religion, or prohibiting the free exercise thereof – – –"
 The wisdom of the founders is clearly expressed in this language. They were, even after the passage of a couple centuries, still very aware of the religious persecution and intolerance their ancestors had suffered in their native countries and the great sacrifices they made when they immigrated to America.
 Most of the first immigrants were religious groups arising out of the Protestant Reformation. That great teacher Martin Luther had lit a fire for religious freedom. Our forefathers did not want government involved in any way in their religion,- promoting , restricting or choosing their faith for them.
 However, by the time of the revolution there was also a large contingent of Anglicans who had migrated from England and who remained loyal to the Church of England. Most of the Anglicans were in the southern

states. They lobbied strongly for adoption of a "state religion.", Anglican, of course. They lost!

Many of the founders were Deists. Many Protestant denominations from New England, New York, Pennsylvania and especially the Baptists wanted nothing to do with having religion married to government. Faith was a very personal commitment. Government had nothing to do with it except to protect every citizen's right to their personal faith or lack there of. They wisely passed the First Amendment.

However, throughout the 19th century and the early 20th century and with some moderation through the remainder of the 20th century, religious-based laws were pushed and quite a few were enacted e.g. censorship, prohibition,

Also in bursts of patriotic religious fervor such phrases as "in God we trust" and "one nation under God" appeared on United States currency and in the Pledge of Allegiance, God Bless America in music almost outshone the Star-Spangled Banner!

Public schools held baccalaureate services and prayer and religious music was commonly used in and at school functions.

However, the United States Supreme Court in several decisions held it violated the First Amendment establishment clause when public schools incorporated religious acts or services of any kind in official school functions, whether in the classroom or other programs.

Catholics, for the most part, had their own private schools. Public schools had mostly "Protestant" student bodies and staff.

Of course, there was a wide disparity of fundamental "Christian" beliefs and practices represented by various Protestant "denominations".

Then there were the minority religions-Jew's, Muslim's, Hindu's, Buddhist's, and sects, Deists, atheists, agnostics, Hare Krishna's, etc. etc. Just drive around the United States and see how many different religious groups places of worship exist. Even small towns have several places of worship for different religious groups.

These decisions of the United States Supreme Court caused a big uproar and still are breached on many occasions. They are also misinterpreted and misapplied by school boards and administrators and teachers who are either ignorant of their meaning or intent, or just want to enforce their own particular beliefs. An example of this would be having a rule in place which denies students, teachers, or other employees the right to pray quietly and privately in public school facilities without distracting from the classroom or other school functions.

In the late 20th century, a revival of the push to have religion and faith play a much greater and integrated part in government at all levels resulted in a strong movement in the political process (especially in the Republican Party, with the Democrats somewhat reluctantly following suit in order not to lose voters) to support allowing religious schools, "charities" and private education and charter schools to be partners in carrying out "government" social and education programs and receive tax money and supplies from the government to do so.

There was already a strong push for recognition of religious activities in government, functions, e.g.:"In God we trust", "one nation under God", Congressional Chaplains, National day of prayer, annual Catholic prayer service, displaying the "10 Commandments".

As opposed to the founding fathers, many current religious leaders and their individual faithful seem to have this great insecurity which generates the overwhelming need to have the power of government support, defend and profess their particular religious beliefs.

On the other hand, nonbelievers and many citizens of faith have a total fear of religion being promoted by government or government adopting a "state" religion.

Tolerance on both sides and amongst each side becomes very difficult when government is introduced into the mix in any way.

Freedom for all can only be maintained by the total separation of government from religious and nonreligious beliefs.

However, the U. S. Supreme Court has in a number of decisions permitted government to use/support charitable and religious owned and operated entities (as long as they do not engage in religious marketing e.g. proselytizing, missionary activities), to help with operating government programs, both federal and state.

Obviously, this government money supports the religious groups infrastructure and outreach.

Mixing religion and the power of government that is designed to protect the freedom of every citizen is like mixing oil and water — both are destroyed! It is impossible to maintain freedom of and from religion if any form of government adopts a religious faith as the "state" religion. Mixing religion and government destroys any chance of either freedom of religion, or from religion, existing.

You can have government that forbids the existence of any and all religious faiths, e.g. communism. Or you can have government that adopts one religion as the "state religion." and forbids the practice of any other religion as the European monarchies did, (e.g. Catholicism and the Pope) and as the Muslim nations do. But you cannot have freedom of religion and from religion where the state government adopts one religious faith. Freedom of a citizen to believe in and practice the faith of his or her choice, or none, cannot survive in a government structure which promotes, supports or declares the validity of one religious faith, or none.

Freedom of citizens to choose and practice a religious faith, or none, must be totally sheltered from government. Our nations Founders recognized this. There ancestors had immigrated to the colonies to get out from under the power of monarchs supported by specific religious groups, especially the Catholic Church and the Pope in Rome!

This freedom can only be maintained if government is totally secular. Religious institutions partnered with government have been, over the history of the human race, the greatest en-slavers of the human race.

Our forefathers, founders of our democracy, were very aware of the history of monarchies and other tyrannical governing powers and their partnerships with religious powers to control and enslave their subjects and maintain their power. These fathers of our country and architects of our Constitution specifically dealt with this issue in the First Amendment to our Constitution quoted above.

Many citizens who are Christians assert that the United States of America is a "Christian nation". Obviously, this would make the government of the United States of America a "Christian government" in total violation of the First Amendment. The United States of America is populated by a majority of citizens who adhere to, profess and believe in the Christian religion. However, there is almost as many, maybe more, denominations/sects of the "Christian religion" as there are other religions e.g. Muslim, Jewish, Hindu, Buddhist, etc.

The majority of citizens of the U. S. who profess a religious faith are Catholics, but even Catholics are not monolithic in supporting the Catholic Church's' beliefs as to government's role in regulating personal conduct e.g.

a woman's right to choose, religion's role in public schools, birth control, marriage, divorce, running government programs supporting education and social safety net programs through religious organizations. There is also broad disagreement amongst Catholics as to the place of women in the church and in society!

There are a number of different definitions of God or the creator. Obviously, our government does not define "God". Government under our Constitution is specifically denied that right.

Human beings as individuals, and collectively in groups, have developed definitions of "God" as humanlike or mystical in many forms solid and ethereal.

The personal faith/belief of each and every citizen must be respected and treated exactly alike by our government, without favor or disfavor toward any or all. Rather government must be totally and completely neutral as to all. Tolerance is not comfortable or easy. Intolerance is easy to justify and practice!

Government does not believe or disbelieve, only human beings believe or disbelieve in a particular faith and belong to a particular religious group or denomination thereof, or have no belief in a religious faith whatsoever. E.g. humanists, agnostics, atheists. By the government placing such sentiments as: "in God we trust" on government currency and buildings, supporting and engaging in a national day of prayer; supporting the work of religious operated charities and charter schools; recognizing the Vatican as a country entitled to diplomatic relations; participating in the annual Catholic sponsored religious service, having religious chaplains serving in the Congress and military, the US government violates the clear injunctions and philosophy behind the First Amendment of the Constitution.

Individual citizens who are elected, employed or appointed to any office in government can believe in any religious faith, or none, and worship in any manor or place, they choose, or none! One would hope that persons serving in government would be persons of integrity, honesty and intelligence who are fully committed to maintaining and enhancing the freedom of every citizen as guaranteed by our constitution.

Case Law

Recent decisions by the United States Supreme Court have whittled away at the concept of total separation of church and state. Some of the cases are:

1986 . Witters vs Washington

Approved use of state tuition grants at religiously affiliated colleges, including grants to students pursuing ministerial degrees.

1988 Bowen vs Kendrick

Held constitutional. The "adolescent family life act" which authorizes federal monetary grants to public and nonprofit organizations, including faith based organizations, for services and research in the area of premarital adolescent sexual relations and pregnancy.

1997 Agostini vs Felton

United States Supreme Court took the unusual step of explicitly overturning two of its strict separation decisions and upheld a government program providing remedial education to students of private religious schools by government employees on the premises of those schools. The court said there was no advancement of religion reasonably attributable to the government!

2000 Mitchell vs Helms.

In this case, the court upheld the state program that loaned education materials and equipment to religious schools in economically disadvantaged areas. The court majority rejected the "strict separationist" theory.

In a concurring opinion by O'Connor and Breyer , they opined that there must be actual diversion of government assets to religious use and not merely the possibility of such diversion.

2002 Zellman vs Simmons-Harris.

The court approved a state program providing vouchers to pay for children in distressed public school districts to attend private religious schools.

2011 Arizona Christian School Tuition Organization vs Winn.

The Arizona law under consideration in this case provided for income tax credits for donations to private organizations which provide tuition grants to students attending private religious schools. In a 5 to 4 decision, the court held that the plaintiffs did not have standing to raise an establishment clause issue because the court would have to speculate as to the effect of the tax credits on the budget of the public taxing entity, thereby avoiding the ruling in FLAST vs COHEN (1968).

The Supreme Court of the United States is now comprised of seven Catholics and two Jews. Five of the Catholics agreed to this decision. The Chief Justice of the court is a Catholic.

These decisions parse and dilute the strength of the First Amendment establishment and free exercise protections for no discernible good reason.

Religious institutions are not required to be a partner in any of the subject programs funded by tax dollars for the programs/policies to be carried out and succeed. The only real affect of participation by religious entities using government money is to unnecessarily mix government and religious entities and chip away at the separation of religion and government.

Seven Catholics on the United States Supreme Court, no matter what their individual political bent or the fervor of their religious convictions/beliefs, is not good. In fact, it is disgraceful.

Justice Thomas is a total disgrace. Scalia with his "original intent" philosophy, which he avoids when necessary, as he does in these cases, is a threat to freedom in all areas of the political spectrum. Justice Alito is scary and his early votes are not comforting.

The ruling by the same five justices in Citizens United, permitting corporate, union and other non political organizations to make unlimited monetary contributions to support political parties and candidates in any amount thru Super Pacs is a total rewrite of the First Amendment free-speech provision. Corporations are not "people". Freedom of speech is clearly guaranteed only to "people" by the clear language of the First amendment. Where is Scalia's "original intent" analysis here?

The court's recent decisions regarding displays of religious symbols, biblical quotations and religious displays on public property are trending in the same direction as the "programs" cases, but do not stray nearly as far. Why? Simply because the issues are not central or important to the support of any "religious program" or entity.

The controversies over the display of the "10 Commandments" in or on government buildings and property are ridiculous and have no rational basis. The 10 Commandments are not the foundation for our legal system/law. They are mostly tenets of Christian/Jewish religious beliefs and rules. If the government actively or nominally promoted them (except as to murder, theft and false swearing) the government would obviously be "establishing" religion!

The court decision in Hossanna-Tabor Evangelical Lutheran Church, rendered in January 2012 re the issue of whether or not laws concerning discrimination in employment applied to religious groups is a correct decision.

The court ruled that the "ministerial exception", which has been ruled to be rooted in the First Amendment's guarantee of religious freedom, protects church's from employment discrimination laws.

The court should apply the reasoning in this decision to zoning cases involving religious groups holding services in homes and other rented buildings, or building places of worship or other religious facilities where there is traffic and other types of interference with the local citizenry. To hold as the courts have held that this type of activity by religious groups can be regulated under zoning laws and other land-use laws is in my opinion, a violation of the First Amendment right to freedom of religion. One would hope that religious groups would respect the rights of other citizens in the neighborhoods and not cause serious traffic, noise, and other interference with the local citizenry. However, the use of zoning and land-use laws can easily be abused and the enforcement of them unequal.

FREEDOM OF RELIGION AND FREEDOM FROM RELIGION ARE BOTH THREATENED BY THIS TREND IN OUR SOCIETY

AND POLITICAL DISCOURSE. IT ALSO THREATENS THE STABILITY, EDUCATIONAL INDEPENDENCE AND FREEDOM OF OUR PUBLIC SCHOOLS FROM THOSE WHO WOULD USE THE PUBLIC SCHOOLS TO PROMOTE THEIR PARTICULAR BELIEFS!!

Chapter Three

CONSTITUTIONAL PARTICIPATORY GOVERNMENT

It is painfully obvious in this year 2012, and has been obvious for decades, that our government has become increasingly dysfunctional.

The basic substantive provisions of the Constitution written by our founding fathers are not the problem. They become more valuable and cherished with the ages. (The Bill of Rights)

However, many of the administrative and structural provisions, and some of the election provisions, no longer work to provide equal protection, equal opportunity, equal representation and maximum personal freedom in our society, which has changed dramatically in many ways since the Constitution was written and adopted.

Our country is vastly larger in area, has hundreds of millions more in citizen population, which is exponentially more diverse in its roots, ethnicity, race, religious affiliation, or lack thereof, education, rural, urban and suburban lifestyles.

We have huge population centers, small towns and villages and vast open spaces all tied together by a transportation system which includes millions of miles of highways, railroads, waterways and an airport and seaport system.

We are connected by a communication system that gives us instant contact almost anywhere in our nation and the world.

We have an economic/business system and infrastructure second to none and wealth, both monetary and hard assets beyond comprehension.

But we still operate in, and govern ourselves through, a political system which is over 200 years old and built to operate in a totally different and exponentially smaller society. The political system has also grown and changed dramatically and grown a lot of warts! This is true especially of the two-party system.

We must retool, re-tune and modernize the rules under which we select and operate our governing bodies if our democracy is going to survive.

In the years since the adoption of our Constitution, but essentially from the end of the Civil War, social, economic and political forces have increasingly fought for changes in the rules or to bend the rules or to favorably interpret the rules to gain greater power and influence in the political process of choosing elected officials and passing laws, all to benefit their special interests. Maintaining power has become the total obsession of the two-party political system. The two parties system along with unlimited terms in office in the House and Senate has made campaign money the political God.

Every citizen should have the right to contribute any amount of money or in-kind service to political candidates campaigning for political office or in support of a political party or group supporting particular candidates or issues being decided in federal, state and local elections.

The number of millionaires who buy seats and serve in the congress is a disgrace. Added to the disgrace is the fact that many of them serve for many terms, even a lifetime. Ted Kennedy is the most disgraceful example. He should have been a convicted felon rather than having a lifetime seat in the Senate purchased for him!

To protect and maintain the integrity of our political system and our democracy ,and freedom of the individual citizen, I propose the following amendments to the United States Constitution.

Only one of my proposals affects a substantive provision of the Constitution. In that regard I propose clarifying the First Amendment re free-speech to reverse the disastrous decision of the United States Supreme Court in the Citizens United case. This decision, if left to stand, is fatal to our democracy and the freedom of the individual citizen, the "people",except for the very wealthy and politically powerful.

Corporations, unions, religious groups, or other business, fraternal and commercial organizations, or organizations with multiple membership of citizens who are not like-minded politically and whose sole purpose is not to support a particular political party, candidate, issue, or law should not be permitted to participate in any manner in the political process. Neither should these organizations be permitted to lobby elected government officials, or their support staff with money or support of any kind. We should make one citizen one vote a true rule of our democratic government political processes.

To accomplish this I propose the following amendments to the Constitution. In making these proposed constitutional amendments I am setting forth outlines, not specific language. There are many excellent constitutional scholars and attorneys who are much more capable than I of drafting specific language to give effect to these proposals.

Article I

Terms of office for Senators:

Section 3 of Article 1 shall be amended to provide that Senators shall be limited to two terms in office with each term in office being six years for a total of 12 years in office. One half of the members of the Senate shall be elected every six years.

Terms of office for members of the House of Representatives.

Section 2 of Article 1 shall be amended to provide that members of the House of Representatives shall be limited to two terms in office, with each term in office being four years for a total of eight years. One half of the members of the House of Representatives shall be elected every four years.

The Senate and the House of representatives shall adopt the rules necessary to carry out the staggered elections. The goal shall be equal representation based on population in both the House and the Senate, essentially as it is for the House at this time. To give effect to this amendment, Section 3 of Article 1 shall be amended to provide that all Senators shall be chosen from approximately equally populated districts without regard to state boundaries. Formation of a Senate district shall take into account common characteristics, e.g. economic, rural, urban, geography, natural resources, and compatibility with neighboring communities in general.

Executive

Article 2 shall be amended to provide that the President shall be elected for one term of six years and be limited to that term.

Article 2 shall also be amended to eliminate the Electoral College.

Article 2 shall also be amended to provide that the compensation of the President shall be as set by an independent commission chosen by a joint committee of the legislature. The compensation shall be in line with the base compensation of the nation's top business Chief executive officers.

Article III
Judiciary
Supreme Court

Section 1 of Article 3 shall be amended to provide that the Supreme Judicial power of the United States shall be vested in one Supreme Court made up of three divisions with nine justices each.

Section 1 shall also be amended to provide that each Justice of the Supreme Court shall be limited to serving one term of 12 years. The Congress shall establish rules providing that the terms of Justices shall be staggered so that one third of the terms shall terminate every four years and one third shall be appointed every four years. Judges of the Federal Circuit Courts shall also be limited to a term of 12 years. Judges of the Federal District Courts shall be limited to a term of eight years. Filling vacancies resulting from resignations, death or other causes shall be the same as presently accomplished.

Jurisdiction of the Divisions of the Supreme Court:

A. Division One shall have jurisdiction of all civil law cases arising out of the United States Constitution and laws of the United States enacted by Congress over which the Federal Courts are granted original jurisdiction by the Constitution or laws enacted by Congress and other civil cases appealed from the lower courts of the United States, including civil cases involving laws of the several states in which a question of their compliance or lack thereof with federal constitutional law or legislative law is presented. Division one shall also have jurisdiction of all civil cases appealed from Supreme Courts of the States.

B. Division two shall have jurisdiction of all issues of criminal law arising out of the United States Constitution and laws of the United States enacted by the Congress over which the Federal Courts are granted original jurisdiction by the Constitution, or laws enacted by the Congress and other criminal cases appealed from the lower courts of the United States including criminal cases involving laws of the several states in which a question of their compliance or lack thereof with federal constitutional or legislative law are presented. Division Two shall also have jurisdiction of all criminal cases appealed from Supreme Courts of the States.

C. Division III shall have jurisdiction of all cases arising out of disputes between the Executive and Legislative Branches of the United States government as to the powers granted by the Constitution to each branch of the federal government and whether or not action or inaction by one department has exceeded, neglected or abused the powers and duties assigned by the Constitution to that branch, specifically, but not limited to, all cases arising out of Sections 8, and 9 of Article 1 and Sections 2 and 3 of Article 2 of the Constitution and Article 4.

Division III shall also have jurisdiction of all cases where the court is asked to decide questions of "states rights" under Amendments IX and X and issues arising under the Commerce clause, Section 10 which come to the Supreme Court through the Federal Court system or from State Supreme Courts.

Section 4 of Article 4 shall be amended to delete "republican form of government." And add in place thereof "government elected by the one citizen, one vote rule" form of democratic government.

Each Supreme Court division shall elect a Presiding Justice from their members to administer that Division.

The collective membership of the three divisions shall elect from the members of the three divisions, who have served at least six years on the court, a Chief Justice who shall administer all three divisions and participate in the decision of cases in all three divisions as he or she deems appropriate or necessary to obtain a clear majority decision.

Cases in any division, which result in a failure to reach a decision or a clear majority, decision, (6 to 3) (5 to 3), shall be submitted by the Chief Justice to the entire membership of the three divisions for a decision.

All original nominations of Justices, which take place after this reorganization, shall continue to be made by the President pursuant to Article 2 section 2 and confirmed by the Senate.

The initial expansion of the membership of the court shall be by nomination of a nominating committee made up of the then sitting President of the United States, the President of the Senate, the Speaker of the House of Representatives, and the Presiding Judges of the Circuit Courts of Appeal of the United States. No one shall be nominated to be a Justice of the Supreme Court who has been active in any political party or movement.

Confirmation shall be accomplished individually by the Senate by majority vote as presently provided. Filibusters shall not be permitted. Each nominee shall receive an up or down vote.

Article One

Section 8 of Article 1 shall be amended to add the following provision:

> The procedural and operating rules of the legislature (Senate and House of Representatives) shall not permit filibuster or other procedural tactics for the purpose of defeating an up or down vote on the matter brought to the floor of the House or Senate for a vote after the required committee hearings, reading, and debate.

The Supreme Court , as originally established , with nine Justices simply cannot handle the many cases raising significant issues and questions of law coming up out of both the criminal, and especially, the civil side, of the lower courts, Federal and State, which are also under staffed.

The powerful get heard and the remainder are left to twirl in the wind!

Too many cases in which significant issues of Constitutional Law are decided result in one vote majority decisions, many with clear politically based arguments on both the majority and minority sides. The Citizens United case is the worst example which followed the previous worst example-Bush v Gore! (Dred Scott is in a class of its own)

The Supreme Court of the United States must also expand with the expansion of the society which it serves. Its original numeric makeup, organization and procedural rules are not cast in stone or essential to maintaining its original function. Its actual ability to perform is!

We have millions of citizens of all ages, educational levels, experience, skills, professions who are capable of doing a good job as members of Congress and learning the job quickly. The old saw put forth by the protectors of the current status quo that we need the experience of professional politicians with long service is simply not true. The civil service was organized specifically to provide continuity and a reservoir of experience, history, and technical knowledge for the elected members of congress to draw on in proposing and drafting legislation. Further the Congress has all kinds of staff and expert advisors in any and all areas of expert knowledge from which to gather the information they deem it necessary to have to make decisions. Professional politicians are not needed and are in fact crippling our Democracy!! PARTICIPATION

Chapter Four

THE CONSTITUTION AND THE DEATH PENALTY EIGHTH AMENDMENT

"Excessive bail shall not be required, nor excessive fines imposed, nor cruel and unusual punishment inflicted-----"

Cruel and Unusual.

"Original" meaning, "intent"? What was the understanding of these words by the original authors of the Constitution?

Certainly, the death penalty has never been considered an "unusual" punishment and would not have been so considered by the original framers of the Eighth amendment. "Unusual" has never been a subject of controversy or discussion regarding the imposition of the death penalty except in the analysis of equal protection issues surrounding the prosecution of death penalty and rape cases.

The issue raised in the late 19th and early 20th centuries was whether or not the death penalty is a "cruel" punishment.

During this same time there was a growing movement which believed that the causes of criminal conduct of human beings could be treated and the causes of antisocial, dangerous , intentional harmful conduct towards other human beings could be cured and offenders rehabilitated and returned to society.

Great emphasis on rehabilitation of those humans convicted of criminal conduct was generated by the social engineers – e.g., psychologists, psychiatrists, therapists and counselors and many programs were set up in the prison system designed to accomplish the rehabilitation and the return to society of persons convicted of crimes of all kinds and all levels of severity.

The Supreme Court's struggle with the Eighth amendment "cruel and unusual" punishment issue began in earnest with the Trap v Dulles case in which the court stated:

"The eighth amendment must draw its meaning from the evolving standards of decency that mark the progress of a maturing society."

This statement was cited by the court in Furman v Georgia in which the court took on the equal protection issues arising out of the prosecution of death penalty cases in Georgia and Texas.

Furman did not deal with the issue of whether the death penalty was "cruel" punishment.

In a bit of convoluted reasoning the court held that the death penalty was "unusual" when imposed in cases where the accused's Fifth and Sixth amendment rights to equal protection and due process were violated. The death penalty was not held to be a cruel, and or, unusual punishment in cases of premeditated murder.

By the back door, it was held to be cruel and unusual in rape cases. However, the principal holding, even in the rape cases, was an equal protection holding based on discriminatory and unequal imposition of the death penalty, the same as in murder cases.

Certainly it was not unusual to have the death penalty applied in rape cases prior to this ruling! For centuries in the previous history of English and United States law the death penalty had been imposed in rape cases.

Morality, Justice, the Courts.
And
The Death Penalty.

A. The death penalty and cruel and unusual punishment.

The death penalty was not a moral issue when our Constitution was written. Cruel and unusual punishment was not thought of as relating to the death penalty. This moral and philosophical approach remained the clear mind set of society and the courts through the 19th and early 20th centuries.

By the mid-20th century the psychiatric medical discipline was gaining respect rapidly and was asserting the ability to cure many aberrant mental conditions affecting human behavior. There was increasing pressure from the intellectual, psychiatric, philosophical, religious and legal communities to have the death penalty declared cruel and therefore a constitutionally prohibited punishment.

The Supreme Court took up the issue in Furman v Georgia in 1972 (408 US 238).

There was clear evidence in Furman that blacks were much more likely to receive the death penalty than whites in cases arising in Georgia and Texas. The Court did find that the death penalty was a cruel and unusual punishment when imposed for rape. In both crimes, murder and rape, the court held that the courts of Georgia arbitrarily imposed the death penalty on black citizens unequally when compared to the imposition of the death penalty on whites in similar factual situations. Therefore, the Georgia and Texas courts had violated the equal protection provision of the V1 Amendment.

Gregg v Georgia followed in 1976 and was also decided on equal protection issues.

Justices Brennan and Marshall dissented and argued that the death penalty had become a cruel punishment based on the advances in modern society, the dissent argument in Trap!

Over the years since the Furman and Gregg cases, the Supreme Court has heard and decided many death penalty cases. Most have dealt with procedural and evidence issues. A few have dealt with cruel and unusual punishment in particular factual situations – e.g., mental retardation and juveniles.

The Supreme Court has required a separate penalty phase in all death penalty cases. The penalty phase must be presented to the same jury as heard the guilt phase.

In the penalty phase the state presents the aggravating factors and the defense presents the mitigating factors. The jury must then find whether or not the state has proven beyond a reasonable doubt that the aggravating factors outweigh the mitigating factors. If the jury so finds, then they may impose the death penalty or recommend it to the court, depending on the applicable state or federal statute. If the jury finds the state did not prove beyond a reasonable doubt that the aggravating factors outweigh the mitigating factors, then the jury must recommend one of the lesser sentences (life without parole, life with parole, life with a fixed number of years before eligibility for parole, as the applicable statute may provide). I have not tried to be legally precise in this analysis, just to demonstrate the basic procedure.

The court requires all of this even though in the guilt phase of a first-degree murder trial where the death penalty is sought, the jury has already found:

1. The act of killing was done by the defendant with intent;
2. The killing was perpetrated by the defendant with premeditation;
3. The defendant killed the victim without just cause, e.g. self-defense;
4. And/or the killing was done by the defendant or a co-defendant in the act of committing a charged felony. (no premeditation is required, e.g., robbery, rape, burglary.)

The jury in the penalty phase always has the right to find the defendant guilty of a lesser included offense, e.g. first-degree murder or second-degree murder. Such a verdict would eliminate the death penalty.

It is obvious that the U S Supreme Court and the State Supreme Court's and many lawyers and state legislatures do not like the death penalty and, if they had any guts, they would just legislate it out of existence, (some have), or the courts would find it to be cruel punishment and therefore barred by the Eighth amendment.

The fact is, the enforcement of the death penalty has become a total mess and a total embarrassment to the legal profession and the courts.

Why?

1. When entered as a judgment of the court, the execution of the judgment takes an average of 10 to 15 years and in many cases longer. This is patently outrageous and cannot be justified.
2. The charging and prosecution of death penalty cases is very inconsistent in local jurisdictions across the country by both state and federal prosecutors.

Deals are made..Many prosecutors, by the use of plea bargaining ,agree to not seek the death penalty if the defendant pleads guilty to a lesser charge.

The reasons given for entering plea bargains usually include either some desire by the victim's family to recover the remains of their loved one, or to get closure for families of other victims for the death of which the defendant has not been charged, or to avoid the trauma of a trial, or the desire of law enforcement to obtain evidence to prosecute other suspects.

These kinds of plea bargain deals in capital murder cases, and specifically in mass murder cases like the "Green River" murders, are, in my opinion, not justifiable. In many capital murder cases, the prosecutors simply are not committed to prosecute death penalty cases for personal reasons and beliefs. They also use the excuse that the prosecution would be so expensive that the local political entity does not want to pay for the prosecution. This latter excuse is usually agreed to by discussions held behind closed doors!

3. The Supreme Court's requirements as to jury instructions in both the guilt and sentencing phases, especially the requirements re mitigating and aggravating circumstances, have made the imposition of the death penalty a totally arbitrary and unequal process which brings about unequal results.
4. The wealthy defendant charged with first-degree capital murder can play all of the complicated legal and practical requirements involved in the death penalty prosecutions to create error and sympathy. They retain the best attorneys and experts. This obviously tilts the justice system in favor of the wealthy defendant even though the state is supposed to pay for the defense of the indigent.

The statutory requirements of the penal codes defining murder in its varying degrees should be radically simplified to charge capital murder occurring in the commission of a felony or in the killing of a law enforcement officer, the same as in any other capital murder.

Given a competent human being, disregarding the stress of the situation, who intentionally and without just cause takes the life of another human being, the penalty should be death. To require premeditation just adds another layer of a mind set which is not a fact subject to proof beyond a reasonable doubt in many cases of cold-blooded murder. If the defendant pointed a gun at another human being and intentionally pulled the trigger and kills the person, there is no difference if he/she premeditated the act or not. The innocent victim is still dead.

"Just cause" for taking the life of another human should be defined narrowly, and shall not include situations of severe emotional or mental distress, e.g. caused by sexual infidelity, whether discovered in the act or later under other circumstances. "Just cause" shall include the mental and/or physical abuse of another human being over time, so as to destroy by fear or other intimidation, the capability of the abused person to escape, or seek help, especially, if in the situation, the person killing the abuser is responsible for the lives of others, especially children.

If the imposition of the death penalty cannot be simplified and enforced equally within a high degree of uniformity, then it should be completely abandoned. The way the imposition of the death penalty functions now is surely a worse violation of equal protection than the racist violations in Furman and Gregg.

Opponents of the death penalty have over the years come up with all kinds of reasons to abandon it completely. The reason most pushed by social engineers is, of course, the death penalty is a cruel punishment.

Then there are the following supporting arguments:

- Life imprisonment without parole is a greater penalty. Yes, it is. Then why impose it? If life imprisonment without parole is a more severe penalty, then it too is surely more cruel than the death penalty.
- The methods used to put a murderer to death are inhumane. Hardly!

- Enforcement of the death penalty is more expensive than enforcement of life in prison without parole. This is a problem of the justice system burdened as it is with the requirements previously discussed, a lot of which are self imposed.
- The death penalty does not deter others from committing murder. This is simply not relevant. Deterrence is not a valid consideration for imposing a death penalty or any other penalty for criminal acts..
- There are too many wrongful convictions of capital murder which result in the defendant being sentenced to death where the defendant is later found to be innocent. Then raise the standard of proof for imposing the death penalty to beyond any doubt and raise the level of performance of law enforcement and the court system.
- There is too great a disparity between convictions of minority races and the white race. This is a problem of the validity of, and fairness of ,the judicial system. There are no clear statistics to prove this argument. This is also a societal problem, not a cruel and unusual problem. It is a potential equal protection problem if it can be proven to be systemic.
- The death penalty is not a humane penalty because in a society which places a high value on life, the death penalty is psychological torture. This is an argument based on religion, just as in anti-abortion arguments. Life in prison without possibility of parole and confined to a small cell imposes a much greater degree of psychological torture. Any penalty involving a prison sentence, loss of freedom, is psychological torture.

There is no justice when mass murderers like Manson, the Green River killer and many others avoid the death penalty by plea-bargaining.

In addition to the changes in the charging elements recommended above, simplify the jury instructions as follows:

1. Require proof beyond any doubt as to whether the defendant took the life of a human being intentionally and without just cause.

2. If the defendant has entered a valid confession, and there is admissible corroborating evidence, then the standard of proof beyond any doubt, has been met.
3. If the jury finds as required by instructions one and two above, then the punishment shall be death.

If the jury finds the defendant is guilty of capital murder in the first-degree then the court shall enter a judgment imposing the death penalty. .
EITHER FIX THE JUSTICE SYSTEMS ADMINISTRATION OF THE DEATH PENALTY, OR ELIMINATE IT!
Additional areas of problems in the present administration of the courts:

Appeals in criminal cases, and in death penalty cases especially, should be required to be much more carefully and solidly based in errors of law or fact than they now are. Attorneys should pay for filing motions, writs and appeals without a substantial basis in the record of reversible error or newly discovered evidence not available at trial-e g-DNA.

The court's, on both the civil side and the major crime side, are becoming more and more the courts of the wealthy and powerful.

There is a real need for more court facilities and more judges, but the courts also need to get back to their roots and let social services be supplied by others. Also, society needs to recognize that criminalizing acts of citizens, the criminalizing of which a major portion of the population does not support, clogs the court system and wastes law-enforcement assets. (E.g. simple possession and use of small amounts of marijuana by adult citizens, seat belts for adults ,no smoking in bars.).

No human activity or inactivity should be made a crime when the criminalizing of that activity or inactivity is not supported by at least 90% of the citizenry.

The enforcement of criminal laws which do not have the support of an overwhelming majority of the citizenry creates all kinds of social and enforcement problems.

Tax money that should be used for basic government functions is bled off for no real purpose or good result. Such laws take away money and assets needed to support schools, social services, and other basic government services..

Law enforcement agencies who resist changes in the criminal law eliminating crimes which do not have the support of 90% of the public should not be given much credence . Law enforcement has totally failed to successfully enforce the marijuana laws for at least 60yrs. They have spent hundreds of millions of tax payer dollars that could have been spent on schools and other public services in that effort. They need to focus their efforts on meth, cocaine, and other hard drugs, illegal and prescription and especially on those who supply controlled substances, including marijuana to minors.

Chapter Five

JUDGES.

The federal and state court systems have been hijacked by attorney Bar Associations and "professional judges." secure in their positions for life.

In the Federal system the Constitution provides that judges on all levels be appointed and serve for life.

On the state level there are varying systems. Only a few states appoint for life. A few others appoint and/or elect and judges serve until they lose an uncontested election. Most states still elect and judges stand for reelection every 4, 6 or eight years. Vacancies which occur during a term are usually filled by the governor appointing for the remainder of the term.

The reality is that, once elected or appointed, most judges serve until retirement or death. My experience as a practicing attorney for 45 years plus, (18+ years in California and almost 30 years in Oregon, including serving over four years as a Circuit Court Judge in Oregon). has led me to the firm conclusion that no trial court judge should serve for more than eight years and no state appellate court judge should serve for more than eight years and they should not serve for more than 12 years total as a trial court and appellate court judge.

State Supreme Court Justice's terms should be limited to 12 years and to not more than a total of 16 years of combined judicial service.

My experience with almost every trial court judge has been that, after six years plus or minus, they begin to lose interest, get short tempered ,or at least find it hard to keep their attention on the matter before them.

They also, almost by human nature, come closer to and rely more on certain attorneys who appear before them. They forget that the attorneys are not the important people before them. They see the litigants and hear them less and less. The most important asset of a Trial Court Judge is the ability to listen, listen, listen, and maintain their attention on the litigants. Trial court judges also have to have a clear and certain grasp of the issues in the case before them. This requires at least reading the file before the hearing or trial starts! The longer Judges are on the bench ,the less most prepare! They keep good relations with Attorneys who support them politically.

Many states have combined the traditional two court system of a general jurisdiction court and a lower limited jurisdiction court.

General jurisdiction and limited jurisdiction courts have varying names in different states, e.g., general jurisdiction courts:
>   Superior Court.
>   District Court.
>   Circuit court.
>   Common Pleas Court.
>   Supreme Court,
> Limited Jurisdiction Courts.
>   Municipal courts.
>   District Court's

Gen. Jurisdiction courts have jurisdiction over:
>   civil cases involving monetary amounts over $10,000;
>   family law – divorce, custody and property division;
>   real property law;
>   criminal law – felonies.

Limited jurisdiction courts have jurisdiction over:
>   civil cases involving less than $10,000:
>   small claims.

Criminal – misdemeanors:
>   Infractions,
>   Traffic

In combining the courts, the legislatures have usually elevated the lower court judges to general jurisdiction status and raised their pay accordingly.

Obviously, handling small claims and misdemeanors does not require the same legal skills or proficiency therein as handling major civil litigation , felony criminal cases and family law cases.

Combining the courts in Oregon was done under the theory that it would make the system more efficient. All it did was create a larger bureaucracy and condense power in a state court administration with the Supreme Court Chief Justice as the titular head and a civil servant court administrator doing the work and making the decisions. The cost of running the local courts has increased in Oregon exponentially without a concurrent increase in caseload .

Limited jurisdiction court cases can be handled by attorneys with only a few years in practice. They can gain valuable experience in controlling and administering a caseload and a courtroom. They can learn the value of listening and who the important people are in the courtroom. The civil litigants and criminal defendants and those harmed by criminal acts are the important people in the courtroom.

After serving for several years too many judges begin over estimating their importance and suffer ego enhancement as a result of the respect they receive and power they wield! As years roll by they tend to forget that they are servants of the public and entrusted with a heavy duty to exercise their power with restraint, respect and humility. Judges must project firm control of the court in a manner which demands and receives respect from all those who appear before the court. Successfully combining these attributes is not easy and becomes more difficult with the passage of time for a lot of human beings serving as a Judge.

Compensation for judges, serving in general jurisdiction courts should be comparable to that earned by the most experienced and qualified attorneys in the area.

However, the judge should not receive any health insurance, retirement benefits or other benefits. Judges should take care of those needs out of their salaries. When the taxpayers pay for these "benefits" the benefits tend to become more important than improving the performance of the courts. I speak from experience in attending judicial conferences!

A big caveat! In the past couple decades the duties of a judge, especially in a general jurisdiction court, have been made much lighter and much less demanding. In the private sector , when your duties, or the skills needed to perform them, decrease or are less challenging, your pay is cut!

There has been a big move in the court system to change the judges traditional role in handling family law cases (divorce, custody, support.) and criminal law cases.

Except for property division, family law cases have been turned over to court support personnel, usually from a family social services agency.

The court determines spousal support and child support but there is usually no contested hearing. The parties fill out financial forms and the court applies the "guidelines" and issues an order or judgment.

In criminal cases the court gets a detailed report and recommendation from Corrections as to the criminal record of the Defendant, including the pertinent facts of the case bearing on sentence, jail, state prison, probation, fines and other conditions, and applies the criminal sentencing guidelines and issues a criminal sentence judgment. The supporting agencies and actions in this procedure have different identifiers in different states.

Pretrial motions can be challenging, but difficult issues occur only in a small percentage of the criminal case load. Capital murder death sentence cases are always a challenge for even an experienced Judge. However, most Judges rarely preside over a capital murder case.

The point is, divorce and criminal cases have always been the most difficult and challenging areas of a Judges duties. For example, dealing with the human factors involved as in the biblical example of Solomon cutting the baby in half, or in sentencing a criminal defendant to a long prison term or death.

With the advice of all of the support personnel, and especially guidelines, the role of the Judge is greatly diminished and the pressure of difficult decisions, "Judgments" re custody, visitation, support and family law cases and sentence in criminal cases is greatly diminished.

It is now, and almost without exception, common to see the Judge setting behind the bench with the computer before him or her, punching facts and information into a computer. The program then spits out the sentence, or the support order, or other decision.

Further, complicating criminal sentencing are the mandatory sentencing statutes put on the books by citizen initiatives reacting to judicial discretion in sentencing. Too many times the mandatory sentence does not fit. However the Judge is off the hook.

In a lot of cases the "wise and compassionate" Judge is not seen or heard. Being a judge can be a very comfortable job.

On the civil side, the courts have become the tool of the wealthy and the large, well financed businesses and other well financed entities.

Small businesses and the middle income class cannot afford the expense of seeking justice in the court system in many cases. It takes forever to get a case to trial.

"Small business" is, of course, an ill-defined category. A lot of today's "small businesses" are pretty well capitalized. Even then they cannot fight the really big boys or the government.

Getting a civil case heard by the appellate courts is almost impossible.

Trial courts use all kind of sticks and carrots to settle or send civil cases to arbitration. Too many times the litigant with a good case gets the shaft. But, say the court efficiency experts, he/she/it, did not end up in as bad a shape as pursuing a court case. They cite the cost of the delays, attorneys fees, expert fees, etc., etc.! However, the court gets good marks for disposing of cases efficiently. Unfortunately the middle income class and small businesses are paying the biggest share of the tax load to support the court system and not getting a fair share of the use.

If we no longer value judges for their human skills e.g. their communication skills, wisdom, and their ability to listen and to speak clearly on a level in parity those of the litigants before the court, maybe we should just turn the whole business over to the computers.

In the drive to level sentences meted out for similar criminal activity and decisions regarding child support we are losing, taking away, the Judges ability to make those difficult decisions in sentencing and family law cases which often do not fall within the parameters of the "guidelines".

In my opinion we need to give the judge more latitude, more guidance and less firm instruction in criminal case sentencing and family law cases.

Human beings given the role of a judge and serving in a system for lengthy periods of time, not only lose their patience, concentration and interest, but they resist change and fail to be the savvy, deliberative, wise person the system desperately needs. Solomon, we do not expect, but skillful, deliberative attentive, courteous, strong, perceptive judges open to change and efforts to improve the system and to improve the performance of themselves and the courts are needed.

No one should be put in the position of a Judge in a general jurisdiction court who is under the age of 40 and , better, even 50! Life is an unavoidable and necessary teacher.

General and limited jurisdiction court Judges should be elected. Attorneys practicing in their jurisdiction should not be permitted to support in any way, except a blind poll, the election or appointment of a Judge. Permitting some appointed elite group to choose Judges just isolates Judges from the citizenry and is much more subject to cronyism and the political power structure. No attorney should be permitted to run for election or seek appointment to a judicial office who has been active in partisan politics. Judicial discipline proceedings should be conducted by State legislatures.

There are hundreds of thousands of experienced attorneys in this nation. A large percentage of those attorneys are candidates to be good judges, in limited jurisdiction courts clear up to the US Supreme Court.

WE MUST BECOME A MORE PARTICIPATORY DEMOCRACY AND THE COURT SYSTEM IS NO EXCEPTION

Chapter Six

THE TWO PARTY SYSTEM
THE TWO PARTY SYSTEMS GENESIS.

The two-party system grew out of the political turbulence of the 19th and early 20th century. Republicans ruled from 1862 to 1912, except for the Democratic regime of Grover Cleveland, who served two terms.

The Industrial Revolution was gaining steam rapidly after the Civil War. Fortunes were being made in railroads, steel and other manufacturing. The industrial and financial barons were interested in building a sound, stable economic, financial and legal system with minimum interference from government.

Laissez-faire capitalism was invented. Free enterprise was the rallying cry and hailed as the economic structure which would lead the country into a future of opportunity for all. The financial and industrial barons loved it. The small business, Main Street, entrepenures also loved it. Everyone believed they would have the opportunity to succeed, become wealthy and live the good life. They did not need government in their businesses or their lives. All they needed was stability in government, not regulation or interference!

The early 19th century heritage of the rise of new political movements and parties to press for government action to meet or change perceived social or economic inequities or problems was no longer desirable or needed.

Intellectuals developed the academic discipline of "political science". They concluded that a two-party system would provide the stability needed by society. It would benefit all classes of society. A science "political science" was not and is not! It was my Major at Ohio U.!

Between the turn of the 20th century and the Great Depression the contest for political power began to sort itself out as different economic, business, workers and social groups sought support from and gave support to one or the other of the Republican and Democratic parties. However, the Republican Party, born out of the anti-slavery movement in the northern U S was also business oriented. The Democratic Party was the "populists" People's party with strong post-Civil War support in the South until the 1960s, when the civil rights movement rose to prominence.

Economic issues were uppermost in national politics in the early 20th century. Relations with the rest of the world were mostly driven by the quest for markets. National pride, bolstered by military strength, grew as a major force in foreign relations e.g. the "Spanish American War,". The concept of the "America's", North and South, as separate from Europe, and our sphere of influence and economic power grew. Europe was told to stay out of the America's.

An isolationist foreign policy developed which included a "don't tread on us" mantra, bolstered by Teddy Roosevelt's "speak softly but carry a big stick". This mind set became the guiding philosophy for participation in world affairs.

The growing population and its concentration in urban areas was creating a number of different social problems. The Republican Party stuck to the business and economic issues. Gradually the Democratic Party began to support programs to meet the social issues that were arising out of the country's rapid growth. Teddy Roosevelt, originally elected as a Republican, became more and more interested in resolving social problems and preserving natural resources. In the years after he left office he became increasingly at odds with the power brokers in the Republican Party and joined the movement to form the Progressive party, which, when he ran as the Progressive parties candidate for President, became known as the Bull Moose party. With the electorate split amongst three parties, the

Republican candidate, Taft, won the election in 1908. The Democratic candidate, Woodrow Wilson was elected in 1912, and served for two terms.

The Progressive party never gained sufficient backing to be a national force and faded away by 1920. However, many of its programs and policies were adopted during the administration of Franklin Delano Roosevelt in the depression years and after World War II. The Democratic Party over the years adopted most of the Progressive party agenda.

The Progressive party was really the last strong attempt to create a broad-based third party political movement. Other efforts to form a significant third party, e.g. those arising out of the civil rights movement in the 60s ,have had little effect on the national scene. The excesses of the free enterprise system with the Republicans in power in the 20s, especially in the financial markets, leading to the "Great Depression" of the 30s resulted in the Democrats occupying the White House from 1932 to 1952. The Great Depression revealed the hard fact that the capitalist/free enterprise economic system was not self regulating and had to be regulated by government to protect the economy from fraud and market excesses which threatened to destroy our Democracy and personal freedom.

Dwight Eisenhower defeated Adlai Stevenson, the Democratic candidate in 1952. The Republican Party had mellowed and became more moderate in its support of unfettered capitalism and opposition to social safety net programs and opposition to regulation.

Republicans did try to reassert their economic/business above all philosophy in 1938 when they took back power in the Congress and were bitten again by a downturn in the economy. However, their strong isolationist foreign-policy was very popular until Pearl Harbor, which dealt them another blow. Dewey's defeat in 1948 by Truman was really embarrassing!

In 1950 the Korean war broke out. The citizenry of the U. S. were not ready for another War. The war was dragging on and no end was in sight after the Chinese entered on the side of the North Koreans.

So, the moderate, President Dwight David Eisenhower, with impeccable credentials in managing military power was the ideal Republican candidate in1952. President Eisenhower's administration guided the country thru the 50s with a strong, moderate, centrist approach to economic and social issues. Social safety net programs and economic philosophy put into effect by the Democrats in the 30s and 40s were mostly left alone by the Republicans. Some were even improved. President Eisenhower laid out his vision for the interstate highway system, which was funded and started under his regime. Building infrastructure was very popular in the 50s.

After Pres. Eisenhower succeeded in shutting down the Korean War , life was very good in the 50s. However, the Soviet Union and China's communist regimes were asserting their power and demanding a greater role in world politics. Their push for power was mostly in Eastern Europe and Southeast Asia. The colonial powers of Europe were losing their grip. World War II had decimated their economic power base and colonialism was no longer a feasible power base. During the 50s the term" domino effect" became the drumbeat reason to stand up to communist expansionism.

When John F. Kennedy defeated Richard Nixon in '60 the Soviet bloc and China thought they had an opportunity to move and pursue their expansionist programs. Fortunately, Pres. Kennedy stood up to the Soviet Union in Cuba. However, the Vietnam problem was not so simple. Kennedy's handling of it is still a matter of debate. There is no conclusion because Kennedy's Presidency was abruptly terminated by his assassination.

Pres. Kennedy's assassination was a severe blow to the American populations psyche. We believed we had left that era in the 19th century! We were better than that! Our nation had been through two world wars, Korea and the Great Depression and there was a great desire and hope for a long period never ending period of peace, prosperity, and a better life for all. The nation mourned the death of this young man and with him the loss of a large amount of the hope for a better future.

The '60s and early' 70s were a turbulent time with the continuing expansion of the Vietnam, Southeast Asia military involvement and the demand by the citizens of color for the cessation of their treatment as unequal members of the human race. By peaceful protest they demanded the government's protection of their civil rights as equal members of the human race and citizens of the United States of America. They had a strong and gifted champion in Martin Luther King, who was assassinated in the late '60s. Robert F Kennedy was also assassinated. This was a very difficult time in our nations history.

Upon President John F. Kennedy's assassination VP Lyndon Johnson became President. He did well in the civil rights fight but he failed in the management of the Cold War, Vietnam and Southeast Asia.

The assassinations of Martin Luther King and Robert Kennedy exacerbated the situation. There was a desperate desire amongst the citizenry for a return to the relative calmness of the postwar '50s. The Vietnam War protests and the rise of the hippie generation with their cries of- down with the Vietnam War, down with the draft, stop the killing of our young men and women, make love ,make peace not war, became the cries of the younger generation heard across the country and in their rock music. Bring back our tranquility and hope for a better future was the cry of the older generation heard in almost every corner of the nation. President Johnson decided not to run again in 1968.

Richard Nixon rose from the ashes of his political career and became the future. He was a symbol of the victory in World War II ,the Eisenhower administration and the 50s when life was good. Nixon promised to do the things necessary to end the Vietnam War and the national turmoil and to get the nation back on track to a better future. Nixon was elected in '68 and was making progress. However, his choice of a vice president and some cabinet members represented a return to the old dog Republican philosophy of government.

Nixon's biggest failure was in not recognizing the enormity of the threat to our democracy raised by the Middle East countries oil embargo of the early "70s. He failed to meet it with strong measures to prevent our becoming more dependent on foreign oil and to reduce that dependency dramatically. No administration since has proposed or accomplished any thing significant to tackle this threat to our freedom.

Nixon's brilliance fell victim to his ego and shallow personal stature. He destroyed himself and his presidency and put the country further into a national funk. Watergate was his Waterloo! His vice president Gerald Ford, appointed after the downfall of Spiro Agnew, was elevated to the presidency on Nixon's resignation,. Pres. Ford never had a chance to do anything except try to calm the nation and the government and tend to everyday business. Inflation was beginning to run rampant. In 1975 the nation looked to elect a person who was not a part of the Washington DC political scene. Out of Georgia came Jimmy Carter, who seemed to be the best candidate to right the ship.

Unfortunately, Pres. Carter became too involved in foreign-policy and did not have the strength in his cabinet to handle the economy. He did create a much calmer atmosphere in the nation.

In Foreign relations he did a superb job with the Israeli- Palestinian problem. However, the national economy was suffering growing inflationary problems due to the long and costly Vietnam war This resulted in ever higher interest rates, a problem which Pres. Carter's administration never found an answer to.

Pres. Carter would have better served the country by concentrating on economic and other national issues. The country was still healing from the 60s turbulence and the Nixon presidency. The citizenry needed a government that was clearly putting their needs and desires first. The final blow to Pres. Carter's term in office came when he was trapped in the Iran Revolution resulting in the occupation of the U. S. Embassy in Tehran and the taking of the whole Embassy staff hostage.

In 1980, Ronald Reagan, whose ebullient personality, positive attitude and superb speaking ability conveyed a positive, upbeat message to the nation and resulted in his election as President.

President Reagan wisely attacked the economy first, specifically inflation. The money supply was tightened and over several years inflation came under control. Those who had bet on the continuing rise in values of real estate went underwater. Ranchers and farmers were hit especially hard. Savings and loans and small banks who had made loans based on the inflated values of real estate suffered huge losses and many went bankrupt.

The result was a recession in the economy similar to the 2007 – 09 collapse in home values, but not nearly as catastrophic. Back then, the government did not bail out anyone or any business. No individual or business which failed was declared to be "too big to fail"!

A recession and high unemployment occurred but the economy and employment were recovering before the end of Pres. Reagan's first term, mainly due to a huge increase in government spending to strengthen the military, including weapons research and development.

On balance, President Reagan proved to be a good chief executive. He appointed highly qualified, strong people to his cabinet.

He took advantage of our country's long " cold war " struggle with the Soviet Union and communism from the Berlin airlift through Korea, Cuba, Vietnam and the constant deterrent to Soviet military power by the service of tens of thousands of soldiers, sailors and airmen who had manned the far-flung lines of defense in Europe and Southeast Asia in airplanes, submarines, missile silos, radar installations, (especially NORAD) for decades. This response to the Communist leaders push for world dominance had severely overtaxed the communist economy's ability to meet the challenge of the economic power of the United States. President Reagan boldly challenged the Soviet Union to change course. He succeeded dramatically.

President Reagan has been given much personal credit for ending the cold war but he would have been the first to recognize the sacrifice of hundreds of thousands of citizens who served in the military and in civilian defense projects around the world and at home during the "Cold War".

Reagan made a few less than salutary decisions in office, e.g. Iran Contra. He stood by Ollie North, Adm. Poindexter and Robert Mc Farland too long when he should have sacked them early on. Reagan's worst decision was appointing Antonin Scalia to the Supreme Court. He also should have sacked Casper Weinberger, who was a talented man but made a bad decision. Reagan left the nation and the Republican Party in good shape. Reagan also failed to address the growing problem of our dependance on foreign oil. He did not realize that this dependance would become the greatest threat to our economy and freedom. Big oil was his friend!

I do not think he recognized the growing strength of the ultra-right wing conservative economic and religious factions in the Republican Party during the course of his presidency. I am also sure that he would be totally dismayed by the current bunch of radical right-wing conservatives running the Republican Party and the House of Representatives.

This group continually takes Reagan's name in vain to support their pre-"Great Depression" economic and social philosophies. I believe he would have totally rejected the actions and policies of the George W. Bush administration.

The downward trend of the middle income class's share of the economic pie began during Reagan's administration. However, I am sure that Reagan did not contemplate that any policy he supported would bring about such a result. I am sure ,however, that the ultra right wing conservatives in the Republican Party who now attack labor unions and push for less government regulation of the economy, knew.

George H. W. Bush was and is a good competent man and was a good President. He unfortunately came into office at the same time the ultra-right wing conservative economic and religious forces were taking control of the Republican Party. These people ended up destroying his Presidency.

Unfortunately, George H. W. Bush did not have Reagan's good judgment in choosing his cabinet and others for government office. He got off totally on the wrong foot when he chose Dan Quayle as his vice president!

His appointment of Dick Cheney as Secretary of Defense and Don Rumsfeld as Chief of Staff, two long time Washington bureaucrats, did not improve his administration to say the least. He also failed to meet the problem of our dependance on foreign oil. He had too many ties to Big Oil!

However, his appointment of Clarence Thomas to the Supreme Court was clearly his worst. Justice Thomas has turned out to be a total disgrace to the court. His alleged treatment of women has nothing to do with my judgment of the man as a Justice of the Supreme Court. He has written very few decisions of note. His ethics are less than satisfactory for a justice of the peace, let alone a Supreme Court Justice. His judicial philosophy is pre- historic!! He is a serious threat along with Scalia, Alito, Roberts and Kennedy to the freedom of every citizen of the United States. When George HW Bush ran for president, I respected him for his World War II service and his long public service from World War II to the present. When he ran for president he was an experienced and smart candidate. However, in retrospect, if I had known he would appoint men like Thomas, Cheney and Rumsfeld , I would not have voted for him.

The rising wave of ultra-right wing conservatives in the Republican Party killed George HW's election to a second term by their failure to support him. A lot of the ultra-right-wingers turned to the Texas businessman, millionaire, egotist Ross Perot who attacked President Bush and ran a third-party candidacy. What's with Texas!!

Bill Clinton and his wife Hillary, with their political savvy, took full advantage of the Republican disarray. As a result, William Jefferson Clinton was elected president in '91. Clinton was defined as a " liberal" but he was really a political pragmatist. He was and is a very smart, competent person with very savvy political instincts. He appointed competent people to his cabinet and lower administrative positions, for the most part.

The ultra conservative economic and religious evangelical factions of the Republican Party were beside themselves. They attacked the Clinton administration in every way they could. They succeeded in gaining control of the Congress in the '94 midterm elections. Newt Gingrich with his "contract with America" led the Republican election campaign. He was elected speaker and proceeded to lead the attack against Clinton and his administration's policies. Under Gingrich's leadership, the Republicans even shut down the government by refusing to pass the federal government budget. However the economy rebounded and Clinton was reelected in' 96.

Clinton's sex scandal broke in 1998 and Gingrich led the push to impeach Clinton. The impeachment effort failed and Gingrich ended up impaled on his own sword. He was censured by a strong bipartisan vote for profiting from his position and fined $350,000. He resigned in 1999.

President Clinton left office in 2000 with the country in the best financial condition since before the "Great Depression". The budget was balanced and large surpluses were predicted for the foreseeable future. President Clinton's biggest failure was in assessing and meeting the growing terrorism threat which had resulted in actual attacks against U S facilities abroad and, most importantly, the attack right here in the United States on the World Trade Center in New York City in 1993.

President Clinton also badly handled the terrorist attack on our troops in Somalia. Our troops had been sent to Somalia to prevent a slaughter of innocents and the starvation of thousands more. When our helicopter was shot down in Mogadishu and our troops were slain and their bodies desecrated in the streets, President Clinton should have immediately given our military forces in Somalia direction to use whatever force necessary to take out the two tribal leaders and all others involved, even if it meant there were serious collateral casualties. Somalia and its people would be better off today and a clear message would have been sent to all terrorists!

In addition, the Clinton administration failed to react adequately to the bin Laden, Al Queda group which was organizing Muslim radicals all over the Middle East and attacking United States facilities and citizens in several countries during the 90s. In defense of President Clinton, he did not have good hard intelligence information coming out of the various intelligence agencies in the government who were not communicating with one another. Further, they had come to rely too much on technology to gather information and did not have enough agents on the ground around the world to gather information, analyze and assess the threat.

Of course, in retrospect, President Clinton's most serious error was in signing the Graham - Leach Act, which repealed the banking regulations in the Glass-Steagall Act, which was passed as a result of the Wall Street financial industry collapse in 1929, leading to the "Great Depression". Under the Gramm act commercial banks were again permitted to participate in investment banking and to use their depositors money to do so. In less than a decade the result was , again, the collapse of the Wall Street banking and investment industry, causing the greatest economic collapse since the Great Depression.

President Clinton also failed to take action or propose any effective program to minimize our reliance on Middle East and other foreign oil!!

The presidential election in 2000 was a national disgrace and, in retrospect, even a greater disgrace and failure of the two-party political system. The barnacles placed in the system by the founders and engraved in stone in the Constitution based on their assessment that they were needed to ensure stability in the transfer of government power had long since lost any basis for their continued existence. Democracy defined by the "one man one vote philosophy" (now one citizen, one vote) was and is preached and praised but is undercut by the electoral college provision in the 12th Amendment of the Constitution and the two Senators per state provision in Article 1, Section 3 . The failure to confront and change these provisions for over a century after it became very clear that they are antiquated and completely in opposition to uncontested principles of democratic government, finally arose out of the ballot box like a snake in 2000 and caused great damage to the country.

George W. Bush was "elected" president without a majority of the citizen vote. The vote in one state, Florida, was contested for over a month over a few hundred votes and technical election procedures, and finally ended up in the courts, first the Florida state courts and then the United States Supreme Court.

The United States Supreme Court with a conservative majority aborted its high calling and disgraced itself with a totally unsupported decision which resulted in George W. Bush being declared the winner and taking office as president of the United States.

The ruling in Bush v. Gore was easily the worst since Dred Scott. The Reagan/Bush appointments of Scalia, Thomas, and O'Connor, joined with Kennedy and Chief Justice Rehnquist (appointed by Nixon) to issue the decision which sealed the election of George W. Bush. Subsequent events have resulted in remorse for in one Justice, it's rumored. The Constitution must be amended to eliminate the electoral college and forever foreclose the Supreme Court from deciding Presidential elections.

Pres. G. W. Bush hardly had time to get settled in the White House when the 9/11 attack on the World Trade Center hit the country like an atomic bomb!

There is plenty of blame to go around for not having sufficient safeguards in place to have prevented this disaster. Pres. George W. Bush cannot be blamed for 9/11. He had barely got his feet wet as President. His administration was still being formed. Certainly the Clinton administration has to be held to a very large part of the responsibility for 9/11. Decisions made by administrations going way back which changed the mission, tactics and tools of the intelligence community, and allowed it to be bifurcated into several agencies and operate without indispensable lines of communication ,can also be included in the blame game. Unfortunately, Pres. G. W. Bush and his administration's cowboy reaction and response to the 9/11 disaster has proven to be much worse than the 9/11 disaster itself. The response to 9/11 and the laissez-faire attitude and actions in managing the economy, especially Wall Street and the banking industry under Pres. G W. Bush, in less than eight years, put the country into the worst economic recession since the "Great Depression" and dealt a crippling blow to an already reeling middle income class.

I have always been convinced that, if either Al Gore or John Mc Cain had been elected President in 2000 ,the U S would not have become involved in the Iraq war or bogged down in Afghanistan or suffered the severe recession of 2007-08. Unfortunately, John McCain became a different person in 2008 and prostituted himself to the ultra right wing economic and religious conservatives and, worst of all, gave us Sarah Palin!!

Our dependence on foreign oil supplies grew and gas prices skyrocketed during the G.W. Bush. Administration.

In addition, the tax cuts for the wealthy and large corporate business entities enacted by the Bush administration enlarged the financial hole in the government's budget. The gross national debt doubled during Pres. G. W. Bush's administration from over 5 billion to over 10 billion. Those figures do not include the budget deficit for 2009 already projected before Pres. Obama took office, and caused by the Bush administration policies. Unemployment went from 5%+/-percent to over 12%, resulting in those parts of the population who could least absorb the financial loss ,being hurt the most!!State and local governments found they were totally unable to meet their budget needs, causing the loss of hundreds of thousands of jobs in the public sector, including teachers, police, firemen and social workers. Their real estate tax base was decimated!!

Millions of middle and low income class citizens have lost their homes through foreclosure and millions more owe more on their mortgages than their homes are worth!

The big Wall Street investment and commercial banks were bailed out by government as "too big to fail." The G. W. Bush administration, led by a Secretary of the Treasury, who was a former President of a major Wall Street investment bank presided over this debacle! As in the Reagan recession of the early '80s, little help has gone to the citizens who have lost everything because of actions or in actions of their government. Individual citizens and small businesses were and are not too big to fail.

George W. Bush was totally incompetent as President. He filled his cabinet with a bunch of incompetent Washington old dog bureaucrats, ex professional politicians and ultra right wing conservatives. A lot of Pres. GW Bush's appointments came from the ranks of people who had served in his father's administration. When 9/11 happened he abandoned his position against nation building and took up with the neo-con foreign policy crowd.

His worst choice was Dick Cheney as vice president. Cheney has no respect for the Bill of Rights. He equates freedom with capitalism/free enterprise and the less government regulation, the better. Cheney's foreign-policy mantra was, the hell with them, the United Nations and any country who disagrees with the U S, friend or foe.

Cheney is undoubtably a leading candidate for the worst person to ever hold a high office in our government because of the influence and power he wielded! Agnew was bad but did not wield the power and influence Cheney did. Cheney wielded more power and influence than any vice president in memory. His arrogance was and is unmatched. His only claim to fame and competence was just being a long-time politician and District of Columbia political hack. It had got him a CEO position with long time defense contractor, Haliburton.

Colin Powell was the only bright light in the whole G. W. Bush administration. Unfortunately, he did not wield any power and was used, fed false info and hung out to dry! Condaleeza Rice was just a caretaker Secretary of State. Cheney ruled !

Pres. George W. Bush is overqualified as a candidate for the worst President of the modern era (1900 to the present). He even beats out Nixon and that is very hard to do. Nixon was without scruples, and lacked personal integrity and obviously committed serious crimes in office. However, he did not leave the country in a disastrous economic recession/depression! He was very effective in foreign-policy, especially in dealing with China and the Soviet Union. Nixon, together with every one to follow him, failed miserably in meeting the middle east oil embargo. George W. Bush is probably a nice, ethical, religious, good person. Just totally and dangerously incompetent to be President of the United States.

There is surely reason to suspect that he was groomed and used by the ultra conservative economic free enterpriser's and the ultra-right wing, religious organizations as their surrogate, stalking horse candidate! He had the name, good old American boy image ,born again Christian, Ivy league credentials. He had served in the military, except when he wanted to pursue his political ambition! He had a successful record in business and as Governor of Texas. But ,was he really in charge and making the executive decisions in these endeavors or was he relying on hired 'Assistants'?

Pres. G. W. Bush's relationship with Karl Rove is hard to explain. His support of Rove and permitting Rove to run the vicious, big lie campaign in 2004 is unforgivable. Using this low-life Rove to run his campaign for a second term calls into question Bush's own integrity.

The attacks on homosexuals, the lies about how religion was being attacked in public schools (children cannot pray!) and the use of fear tactics to exploit these and other concerns of the lower and middle class income citizens to get them to vote against their real interests in reversing the decline in their job opportunities and earning power and the protection of their basic freedoms, especially religious freedom, from government interference was despicable.

.Pres. G. W. Bush and the Republican Congress had created programs and passed laws and administrative rules to permit religious and charitable based organizations to receive government money and other assistance to run government social and education programs. The theory was and is that these private groups could more efficiently administer the programs. The right-wing majority on the Supreme Court has upheld almost all of them. Pres. G. W. Bush organized the "Faith Based" office in the White House to work with religious groups.

True conservatives, as I have understood that definition over years, protect the freedom of individual citizens and realize the danger in any grant of government authority or tax dollars to private religious, education, charitable or other private entities to operate , manage or facilitate in any way government created programs. Government support of any private entity to run government programs supports the private entities overhead and infrastructure used in operating and promoting it's private beliefs and programs. These private programs can be and are often in support of controversial efforts to reverse Supreme Court precedents interpreting Bill of Rights freedoms. This obviously creates an unconstitutional use of tax dollars, whether tax dollars are given directly from the treasury or as a tax credit of some kind.

THE TWO PARTY SYSTEM FORTIFIED BY THE LACK OF TERM LIMITS IS THE SINGLE MOST SERIOUS THREAT TO OUR DEMOCRACY AND MUST BE ELIMINATED BY THE CREATION OF A BALANCING THIRD PARTY -MAYBE TWO- AND THE ADOPTION OF TERM LIMITS FOR ALL POLITICAL OFFICES.

Chapter Seven

EDUCATION AND THE PUBLIC SCHOOLS

The public school system, especially the K through 12 schools, has come under increasing criticism in the past two decades. The K – 12 schools have been, and are the target of parents, teachers, professors, politicians, the Federal Department of Education, State Departments of Education, religious groups, anti-religious groups, each with different perspectives, philosophy, criticisms and solutions. Professional administrators, who have their own views, are pummeled from every side. Most are committed, competent people. Some are the "just let me get to retirement" types and a few are totally incompetent and could care less.

How did we get here? Why "we"? Because we are almost all educated by or in one way or another dependent on, or affected by, our public education system. We are parents, students, teachers, administrators, employers, all with an interest in our public school system.

Our public schools, specifically K-12 have grown over the past 125 years from a lot of rural one room school houses with one teacher and 1st to 12th grades with kids in every grade, or almost every grade, to separate grade schools, middle schools and high schools with hundreds of students. The one room schools were run by the students parents or grandparents, and supported by a local tax and a lot of in-kind services.

Participatory Democracy Or Descent Into Oligarchy

The larger cities generally had school facilities housing all students but segregated into grade school, middle school and high schools with hundreds to several thousand students attending one school.

In the early 20th century a low percentage of students were attending and graduating from high school. Curriculum in public schools was comprised of basic subjects, the three R's.

As our nation moved from an agrarian economy into an industrial economy, the demand for a more skilled workforce led to the public schools changing and expanding their curriculum to better prepare students to compete for jobs and fill jobs with different skills.

In the 1920s and '30s there was a large push to build bigger and better school facilities, to consolidate many of the small rural schools and also to make high school available to all students. The larger cities built separate high schools. All included sports with supporting athletic facilities. Every Township and/or town, if large enough, became a school district. The curriculum offered was improved in all schools.

My older brothers were amongst the first generation to benefit from this investment in education. They moved from a one-room schoolhouse to a large brick multi-room building with a cafeteria, gym, playground, baseball field and administrative staff offices.

Our parents and the whole community were very proud. Almost every family participated in supporting the school in some way. They served as school board members, in the PTA, in money raising functions, cafeteria, festivals, plays, farm events (corn husking B's.). There was a strong vocational agricultural program. We were bused to school if we lived more than a mile from school. Lunch was very inexpensive. A student could help in the kitchen and lunch was free.

Unfortunately, this school facility is now and has been for a long time, a rotting hulk, loaded with too much asbestos insulation to be worth saving and too expensive to demolish!

In the early 20th century, and until after World War II, teacher tenure was not an issue. We had a few good teachers, some average and too many not very good.

However, nine of us brothers graduated from high school between 1932 and 1955. One brother quit school in his senior year to join the Army in World War II! Our parents were very proud. We all have had a very good, successful life and raised great families in spite of growing up during the Great Depression, World War II and the Korean War.

Not every young person was so lucky in the '30s, '40s and '50s. If you were not bright enough to make passing grades or did not have parental support (e.g., you had to work on the farm!), or you had some kind of handicap or in some cases, was just the unlucky victim of prejudice,(social, race) or you were judged by the administration and/ or staff to be "slow", you just dropped out! IQ tests were not available at the time.

If you were a girl, and you were unlucky enough to get pregnant, you just dropped out of sight, were sent to a facility far away, often never to return. If the girl returned, it was rarely with the child! Religion, religion, religion! Sin and saving face! Religious activities and programs were an integral part of school.

No one, outside of their family, worried about or thought of developing programs to meet the needs of the mentally or physically handicapped. Their care was up to their families or public institutions – asylums!

After World War II, and picking up momentum in the 50s, change and growth in almost every area of our society occurred with what then seemed like lightning speed. The G.I. bill resulted in the mass university education of a lot of World War II G I's.

Research and engineering created new advancements almost every day. The medical profession produced vaccines and great advances were made in airplanes, automobiles, communication systems and electronics.

Society was changing rapidly. The World War II generation demanded more of the economic pie. Unions grew and pressed for higher wages, benefits and a place at the decision-making table. Teachers also pushed for better pay and working conditions, and more job security – tenure. In the '60s and '70s this push by the middle-class for a greater share of the economic pie continued unabated.

Better and bigger homes, cars and toys was the goal of almost every citizen. This press to live the "good life" required ever greater income to finance the necessities and the good stuff-- bigger homes, cars, boats, vacations, college education and retirement.

Then in the '80s, the bubble began to burst. There had been a growing trend in the 60s and 70s for wives to work and produce a second income. Beginning in the '60s there was growing competition from other nations who, mainly due to cheaper labor, could produce many of the products traditionally produced in our factories for a lot less money..

Good paying jobs for the middle-class began to disappear. This created an ever increasing need for the female partner in the marriage to produce a second income. With both parents working to produce the income necessary to maintain the lifestyle that the middle-class had become accustomed to, the traditional role of the mother in parenting the children changed dramatically. Babysitters and child care providers became necessary substitute providers of traditional parental care. This lifestyle obviously decreased the time and energy parents had to give the needed attention to their children's development, specifically, to provide a nurturing, secure, loving, teaching atmosphere where love and discipline can be given consistently.

This lifestyle also robbed the parents of time and energy to participate in community activities, politics, churches, and especially public schools which is the concern of this chapter.

Over the years, administrators and teachers have, almost by default, become the power and decision-making group in operating our public schools. This is, obviously, not good. I am sure most administrators and teachers would agree.

Our school populations are too large in the urban/ suburban areas in most cases. Large student populations may generate financial economies, but they do not create nurturing, secure, pleasant learning environments with the opportunity for all students to participate in the classroom and in normal interaction with the student body and in extracurricular activities.

Most of the problems in our public schools, result from problems in our society. Brilliant statement! Huh!

The real and perceived ills in our public school system have been taken advantage of by all kinds of critics and groups with axes to grind. There are attacks on the public schools by conservative and ultra-right wing conservative religious groups who allege that public schools attack their religious beliefs and refuse to let their children pray in school or engage in group religious activities . They push for laws permitting them to organize private schools and to use public tax money to support their private schools.

They take advantage of criticisms of the curriculum, teachers, administrators, test scores, graduation rates, being made and used by headline seeking politicians and education experts to support their demand for public tax money or assets. They support the election of people to school boards who are just negative with some ax to grind. They even go as far as the arrogant, right wing religious Texas school board and demand the teaching in public schools of the "intelligent design theory" as the source of the universe, our earth and the human race!

The Supreme Court of the United States as discussed in a previous chapter, has held constitutional the diversion of government tax money and supplies purchased by tax dollars to some of the religious schools and charities.

These religious groups also fight the provision of a healthcare curriculum, which includes birth control and sex education, for both girls and boys.

They also oppose the schools offering science classes teaching evolution, the age of the earth , the history of the earth's formation and the history of the development of mankind.

The demand for this kind of curriculum is hard to understand in this time, which is touted to be an age of rapid advancement in mankind's knowledge of the world and universe in which we exist, truly an age of enlightenment. If there is a creator/God of some form or gender, one has to wonder why that "creator", "God" gave humans a brain if we are not permitted to use it.

Our public schools need to be, and can be, improved to meet the needs of our rapidly changing society. Needed changes and improvements can only come about with significant participation and input by parents. This is a continuing, normal process and nothing new.

Improving the ability, proficiency, and professional training of teachers can and should be a continuing priority. However, teachers are not the principal problem in most of our public schools.

Teachers must give up tenure. Tenure has become an unnecessary distraction to solving real problems. The reason for tenure disappeared long ago. At this time tenure just gives the uninformed a basis for false reasons to blame teachers for all the problems in our public schools. Tenure has become the shield for incompetent teachers. Tenure is no longer needed to protect teachers jobs.

I served over six years on the board of a large school district in California in the late '60s and early '70s, several years as board president. The greatest frustration was the total inability to dismiss incompetent, nonperforming teachers and administrators. The second greatest frustration was parents demand for busing ahead of the need to provide and improve the education of their children. Providing child care surpassed education. I am sure that is just as true today in many school systems.

We need to attract better qualified people into teaching and pay them well. The school year needs to be expanded to eleven months with the usual holiday breaks. If schools are in session eleven months a year, there will be no need to require students to be in school before 9 AM or later than 4:30 PM. The studies are clear that we start school too early. Homework should be limited.

Providing our children with the education they need to compete for a decent job is an exponentially more complex challenge than it was 50 years ago. We no longer live in a mostly agrarian society where the farm families needed their children home during the summer months to work on the farm! Most important, our society needs to reorganize and re-prioritize our way of life. We desperately need to create a societal/economic system where one parent can provide a decent, secure, comfortable living, at least through their children's formative years. (Zero to 16?). This, even if we can no longer drive big, high horse-powered, gas guzzling cars, trucks, boats and RV's This, even if we can no longer live in 3000+ square foot homes. The opportunity for the middle class to earn a decent living must be restored.

Again, our public schools are not the problem. Our societal/political system is the problem. I am convinced that we , as a free society, can only fairly and equally provide a high quality education for all of our children through a public school system that is given full and committed financial, family, community, and professional support and participation.

Kicking the public schools problem up to the State and Federal level is no answer. Parents through local school districts should have the prime responsibility for the education of their children.

School administrators should look to the colleges and universities education departments for ideas and programs to improve teaching skills and curriculum. The school administrators should bring suggested improvements to local school boards for review and approval or rejection.

The nay sayers, citizens with axes to grind and those who would make the public schools into instruments to promote and teach their particular religious curriculum have to be drowned out and defeated by the citizens who just want the best secular education available for their children and are content to leave their children's religious education to the home and church.

I have long had problems with Federal government intervention, both the executive and the Congress, in the public schools. The Federal Department of Education should be doing nothing but distributing federal tax funds to local school districts to level out the public education funding behind every child and making monetary research grants to universities and other secular research groups.

Programs like "no child left behind" simply present a "one solution fits all" answer, an impossible goal, which is doomed to fail a large percentage of our children. They ignore the fact that children's academic abilities cover a wide range. We have the knowledge and tools to meet the needs of every student. Quit emphasizing academics so much that children who are not academically gifted, but have other talents, are made to feel inadequate and failures and drop out. Provide a curriculum that meets the skills of every child and prepares them for the adult world. The availability of on- line courses makes it possible to provide many levels of educational opportunity. Keep them interested and challenged-not bored! Make sure kids-young adults- have time to have fun, be young and without pressure and suffocating structure!

Again, parents (including grandparents, aunts, uncles and cousins) should run our children's schools. If families do not participate in a significant manner in the operation of our public schools, those schools are going to suffer and fail to provide the education we should demand for our children!

There will be schools which will fail or have serious problems because of apathetic parents, or the election of nut cases as majorities on the school board, some of whom just want to destroy the public schools. All public schools will never be made to perform to an acceptable level, but I am convinced that a larger percentage will perform to an acceptable level if they are controlled on a local level by committed parents and families.

PARTICIPATION, PARTICIPATION!

Chapter Eight

IMMIGRATION IN 2012

Immigration has become a political football and a pawn in the fight for political power. We have a federal immigration law which is not being enforced and has not been for years! Why not? There are obviously powerful forces in our society who do not want the law enforced.

Immigration was not a big, contentious issue until the '80s. Illegal entry into the country had become a problem in California (and to a lesser extent in the other border states of Texas, New Mexico and Arizona). The problem mainly involved farm laborers from Mexico and other South American countries. By the mid-80s we "suddenly" discovered that there were millions of people living and working in the country who had entered the country illegally. Most were Latinos from Mexico and South America. A large number of these illegal's were using and burdening our social service safety net programs, schools. Our southern border was not secure at all.

Large agricultural businesses and other industries which use a lot of unskilled labor favored this situation and opposed any change in the status quo. In addition, there was a lot of political pressure from the Latino community, liberal human rights organizations and religious organizations, especially the Catholic Church, to grant a path to citizenship to many of the illegal's.

However, states and local government entities were experiencing increasing financial problems in dealing with the ever increasing demands on social services, schools and law enforcement caused by the illegal's. Demands for help from the federal government by state and local governments to meet these problems was increasing rapidly.

The vast majority of the citizenry of the U. S. were stunned when the extent of the problem became known. The recession of the early '80s put additional stress on public services, local and State Government budgets and employment opportunities. Public demand for a solution from and by the federal government became a politically unavoidable issue. There were loud demands by many segments of the population to close the border with Mexico, stop the illegal entry and to deport all the illegal's..

Unfortunately, the problems involved in identifying and deporting the huge number of illegal's in the country were tremendous and very complicated.

Why complicated? Because of the uncertainties as to whether or not the illegal's had the protection of the Bill of Rights and other civil rights laws, together with the strong support of the illegal's from Latino, religious, human rights groups and the businesses who are profiting from the cheap labor. The people supporting the illegal's were pushing Congress for amnesty provisions for a number of categories of the illegal's.

The 14th amendment to the Constitution provides that every person born in the U. S. is a citizen. Therefore, every child born in the United States to persons, whether to legal citizens or illegal's, is a citizen of the United States. Many illegal couples were parents of children born in the United States. These children are United States citizens and cannot be deported. If their parents choose to leave their citizen children in the US when deported, those children are separated from their parents and, if not taken in by citizen relatives, or others, become wards of the state and a burden on the taxpayers.

Many of the illegal's were and are Catholic. The plea of the religious community is that it is .immoral to cause children to be separated from their parents. The Catholic Church is joined in this position by a lot of other religious and human rights groups .

Who caused this problem? Obviously the illegal parents caused the problem. The citizens of the United States did not! It seems reasonable to ask why the illegal parents of these children cannot be required to take their children back to their native country with them or pay for their support here, or give them up for adoption. No citizen parent in the United States can avoid their parental responsibility.

Second, all kinds of arguments are raised by Latino, religious, and human rights groups and employers urging the passage of immigration laws which provide legal paths for illegals to gain the right to reside in the United States legally and for some, the right to gain citizenship down the road. In the '80s, Congress passed some amendments to the immigration law which provided some of the requested paths for illegal's to gain legal residence. The justification or rationalization was that deporting all of the illegal's was just too huge and complicated a task. It was much more reasonable to just clean the slate and start over. To calm the deportation demands of the citizenry, Congress and the Reagan Administration promised to henceforth fully enforce the new immigration law by providing sufficient funding to secure the southern border. Border security would be tightened and illegal entry stopped and all would be well! Unfortunately, Congress never provided the funds to expand the border patrol or do the necessary improvements to border security facilities to enforce the new law. Therefore, 20 years later, the problem has repeated with a vengeance!

The acts of terrorism accomplished on our own soil in the Clinton years , 9/11, and the continuing threat of terrorist groups committing terrorist acts in the United States together with the drug and arms trafficking across the border with Mexico has elevated the problem exponentially. The estimates are that we now have somewhere between 11 and 20 million illegals in the country! The cry again is that the problem is too large and complicated to identify and deport a large majority of the illegal's, let alone all.

Further, the politicians and the "open border" advocates now assert that the border cannot be totally or even mostly secured!

However, we can and have spent almost $1 trillion in military actions in Iraq and Afghanistan, for no visible or definable increase in our security, but we cannot secure our own borders! This is political BS! Fact is, there is no political will amongst our current politicians to do so.

Every illegal in the country creates demands on all levels of government, on resources of all types, on all aspects of society and thereby decreases the freedom of every legal citizen, to an even greater degree than legal immigration and the growth of our own population.. There are those who make a case for decreasing substantially legal immigration under our current law because of the economic problems we are experiencing. The resources of this country and the planet we live on are finite. We need to face that unalterable fact!

we need a sane and enforceable immigration law. Businesses who hire illegal's should be fined, in relation to their size, an amount that hurts their bottom line. Religious groups that hide or assist illegal's should lose their tax free status and be fined enough for it to hurt.

Degrading the quality of life and freedom of our citizens is a poor and unnecessary path to follow. Already the lower and middle income segments of our citizens are suffering significant loss of quality of life, and most frightening, loss of freedom. But not the wealthy!

When will the LATINO/HISPANIC heritage citizens become just American citizens? My heritage is almost pure Dutch but I am an American citizen first ,last and always!

I would support an immigration law that would provide :

- All illegal's who have resided in the U S for less than 5 years must be deported, no exceptions.
- Illegal's who have resided in the U S for over 5 years and have been law abiding , taxpaying persons, can be granted Green Cards or other temporary visas, documents, which permits them to reside and work in the U S and are renewable every 5 years on meeting the same conditions. They can apply for citizenship through the regular legal channels.
- Illegal's who have resided in the U S for over ten years and have been law abiding, tax paying persons can be granted permanent residence providing they remain law abiding . They can also immediately apply for citizenship based on special conditions e g , contributions to their community, and sponsorship by U S citizens or groups.
- Any action , direct or indirect, by any one in the last two categories, to assist anyone in illegally entering the U S, or to hide illegal's, would be grounds for immediate deportation.

- This program would be strictly conditioned on the establishment by the U. S. government of a Border security system designed to prevent most illegal entry and to immediately deport all illegal's caught in the U. S. The system would have to be supported by a funding source sufficient to carry out its objectives.

The children of citizens whose ancestors have for generations, in war and peace, shed blood, sweat and tears to protect and advance freedom and the good life should not have to compete with illegal's and their children for the bounty of that inheritance!

I would, and I believe most citizens would accept and support an immigration law which could and would be enforced. We are and must be a nation of laws.

Chapter Nine

FOREIGN POLICY.
&
INTERNATIONAL RELATIONS

The United States needs to carefully define and enunciate our foreign policy objectives and how we will project those objectives.

Foreign policy of the United States has increasingly lost connection with reality, specifically as to: 1) furthering the legitimate interests of the citizens of the United States and 2) being a force in the world arena to influence and aid the people of other nations to attain what we view as their inalienable rights as human beings, and 3) promoting the long-term interests of the United States by creating a more stable, peaceful world community.

The United States has increasingly, throughout the 20th century, and especially since World War II, acted alone, or with little support from other nations, to meet international problems which we view as threatening our security or important interests, as well as those of the broader international community.

First, we need to affirm our commitment to work with and through the United Nations to promote a peaceful and secure world order. However, while doing so we must make it clear that we will not support or participate in any United Nation action or program which is not in the best interests of the United States domestically and/or internationally.

The United Nations has become a bloated bureaucracy which, often, either does not act or whose actions are not in line with the interests and or the beliefs and principles of the United States of America .

The United States should build strong alliances with the nations of the world who have stable elected governments, strong free societies and basic common goals with us and amongst themselves: e.g., the European Union and NATO countries, Canada, Japan, India, Australia, Brazil and South Korea. Hopefully Russia and China would come along sooner or later. The U S should work through those alliances to maintain world peace and to continually raise the freedom and standard of living of all human beings.

The United States and its allies should step in only when an independent country steps outside of its borders to conquer or control another country or a despotic regime is committing genocide or mass murder of it's own citizens. Syria at the moment?

However, the United States must at all times retain the right to defend our borders and our citizens from attack and to take out anyone, or group anywhere who attack the United States at home or abroad if the country where the terrorists are based or trained fails to eliminate them after clear demand and warning, e.g. Al Qaeda in Afghanistan, Yemen or anywhere else.

To paraphrase Teddy Roosevelt, the United States should:

> Walk softly, speak softly, do unto others as you would have them do unto you, but, carry a big stick to deal with those who do not give you the same respect and attempt to do or do you harm and let all know what the policy of the United States is without apology.

The United States should absolutely not engage in "nation building", or promoting democratic government unless invited and then only by peaceful means!

The use of our military to promote and carry out foreign-policy should be very limited, , except in striking those who have directly attacked United States citizens within the United States or abroad.

The use of ground troops should be limited to those situations where air power and tactical weapons would not be effective or the amount of probable collateral damage would not be acceptable. The Obama administration has just recently announced a major shift in strategy for the use of our military and in the configuration of our military to meet new challenges.. It sounds like they intend to carry out just such a policy as discussed above.

However, if terrorists are hiding behind their families and countrymen, then warn them to stop or there will be strikes to take them out where ever they are, despite collateral injury, and death.

Iraq is a prime lesson. First, the basic justification for invading Iraq was totally flawed and this glaring fact should have been apparent to the Bush administration.

Second, we did not build an international coalition to join and support our military action. There was never a clear enunciation of our security or other interests. Especially none backed by good intelligence.

France, Germany, and other European nations would not support our actions in invading Iraq and they were right.

Unfortunately, Great Britain was led by Tony Blair, who was as incompetent and ineffectual as George W. Bush.

Osama bin Laden and Al Qaeda must have been giddy with their good fortune in causing the United States to get into the Iraq war and burn billions of dollars for no real benefit. Another result which bin Laden must have loved was the increase in the price of oil from which he received a lot of his financial support and which cost our citizens and economy billions. Bin Laden must have laughed his blank off all the way to the bank!

France was especially vilified by a large majority of our citizens who were misled by the Bush government. When it was discovered that our own government was wrong and there was no truth to the line we were fed that Saddam had nuclear weapons or other weapons of mass destruction, or the capability to produce and deliver them, you did not hear any apologies being made by our government, or the citizen critics to France, Germany and others for the unfounded criticism of their opposition to our arrogant actions in Iraq and the Middle East!

The U. S. should never enter a war which will require a large military commitment without first activating a draft subjecting all qualified citizens to service..

The Iraq War would never have happened if a draft had been put into place or, at the very least, the military action would have ended in short order.

Professional "hired" armies have led to the downfall of many civilizations. History has proven many times over that you cannot hire others to risk death or injury to defend your freedom! In a democracy, everyone should bear the cost of Freedoms defense, especially the human cost.

Agreements made by the GW Bush administration, provide that we will pull all of our Armed Forces out of IRAQ by December 31, 2011 unless the Iraqis request that we stay. Fortunately, they did not.

We should have pulled out of IRAQ even if they requested us to stay. If Iraq is not ready by now to take over their own government and security, they never will be. And, as stated above, we should not be in the business of nation building. The amount of money we have wasted in Iraq is outrageous. We never had a chance to gain any measure of return from our misguided invasion of Iraq in any event. The lost money is one thing, but the lives of our men and women and the broken bodies is beyond tragic. GW Bush, Cheney, Rumsfeld and their pack of neo-con interventionist should not be able to sleep at night. History will judge them harshly and deservedly so.

Concerns are raised by the military establishment and the Republicans and some Democrats in Congress that Iran will invade Iraq. As stated above, the U S should clearly and firmly warn Iran that any invasion of IRAQ by IRAN will be met with an overwhelming military response by the United States with air and sea power and tactical weapons of all types (except nuclear) and we will destroy their military and infrastructure and we will not participate in any rebuilding !

Israel

Israel has become another foreign relations problem in the Middle East.

After the end of WWII and the full exposure of the atrocities carried out by Hitler's Nazi regime with the clear purpose of eliminating by mass murder every Jew from all of Europe, and elsewhere, there was a groundswell of support for caring for the surviving Jewish people and finding a way to provide them with a secure place to live where they would have opportunity to rebuild their lives, families and fortunes.

(Several of my brothers, who served in Europe from the summer and fall of 1944 to VE Day in 1945, had personally seen the death camps.)

Re-settlement proved to be a difficult problem. A movement to relocate the Jews to their ancient homeland, in what was then Palestine grew rapidly. However, Muslim Palestinians occupied most of the area and had for centuries. Only a small population of Jews were still living in that area.

The British, who had militarily occupied much of the Middle East including Palestine for decades, were opposed to this relocation. The British recognized that moving a large number of Jews into the area would undoubtedly cause major conflict between the Palestinians and the Jews. The British tried to keep the Jewish migration out by closing the access routes. However, the flow became a flood and armed conflict broke out between the Jews and Palestinians with the British caught in between.

My recollection is that there was a lot of sympathy in the United States for the movement of the Jews into Palestine. The movie "Exodus" portrayed the conflict and the success of the Jews in carving out a part of Palestine as a homeland. Exodus was a powerful message in favor of the Jewish people regaining a homeland of their own.. The United States supported the Jewish resettlement with material and money.

However, the other Muslim countries of the Middle East were not pleased with this movement. They were mostly mad as hell and vowed to throw the Jews out! So began what is now over a half century of conflict. Through several wars Israel expanded it's borders, including most of Jerusalem.

During the "Cold War" Israel became a valued ally of the U S. Support in the United States for Israel grew until the United States committed to defend the existence of Israel against everyone. The United States has for years supplied Israel with military weapons and supplies and a large annual monetary subsidy.

The solution to the problem of the Palestinians who were dispossessed of their land and homes festered on. Millions of Palestinians were and are now confined to the Gaza Strip in very crowded, terrible conditions without hope of improvement.

Pres. Carter did succeed in putting together a peace agreement between Egypt, Syria, Jordan and Israel in 1979. It did not solve the primary problem of the Palestinian people's demand for the return of their land, especially the parts lost in the 1967 conflict.

Yasser Arafat became the leader of the Palestinians, and remained so for several decades until his death in 2004.

In the years between the 1967 conflict and the death of Arafat, Israel had continued to build housing and full communities on land which, under the 1969 agreement belonged to the Palestinians. Israel also continued to press for complete control of Jerusalem.

Arafat pressed for a separate, independent Palestinian state and the return of all of the land occupied by Israel since 1969. Arafat demanded the cessation of Israel building, housing, etc. on what was Palestinian land under the treaties ending the wars.

Israel, and Palestine under Arafat, seemed to come close to a peace deal in the late 1990s, but it foundered on the Palestinian demand for an immediate establishment of their own country and a solution to the incursions into Palestinian land by Israel. Israel refused to accept an independent Palestinian state or to give up much of their incursion into Palestinian land!

When Arafat died , the chance of a peace agreement died with him. The militant Hamas group and others gained control of the Palestinian government. Other Muslim revolutionary groups increased their power and support for the Palestinians, especially in Lebanon and Syria. There has been intermittent conflict ever since and no real progress toward a settlement of the issues.

Israel continues to move into Palestinian land and build communities. Israel also continues to refuse to accept an independent Palestinian state, or to give up Palestinian lands upon which they have built settlements.

In the last several years, Israel has given majority power to the conservative and ultra-conservative parties who have elected Netanyahu as Prime Minister.

In spite of increasing international pressure on Israel to accept a two nation solution and retreat from all or most of the settlements they have built on Palestinian land and give up that part of Jerusalem occupied by Palestinians, Israel holds fast in its refusal to negotiate on these issues.

The United States should come down hard on Israel. Israel is no longer an essential or even very helpful ally on the international stage, if they ever were. The United States should quietly and firmly advise the Israelis that unless they agree to a two nation solution and other reasonable compromises re Jerusalem and the settlements the U. S. will:

1) cease all monetary and military assistance;
2) withdraw our absolute commitment to defend Israel under all circumstances and to guarantee the continued existence of Israel as a nation.
3) the United States will only guarantee to defend Israel if a two nation solution is reached.

Israel will never have peace and a reasonable guarantee of a secure future for it's children as long as the Palestinians are locked into the Gaza Strip and other small portions of what was their land for centuries. Israel cannot hope to keep major numbers of Palestinians living under Jewish rule. Many Jewish citizens of the United States support a two nation solution.

Jerusalem should be made an international city with a government composed of Jews, Palestinians, the other Middle East Muslim nations, and representatives from Western Christian nations who could be appointed by the United Nations from neutral nations. Jerusalem is a "Holy City" for Muslims and Christians as well as Jews.

The United States needs to strike now and take advantage of the strong movements for freedom in the Middle East Muslim countries. Hopefully by doing so we can build respect for United States leadership and bring hope for a better future for the whole region.

The United States should refuse to deal with Netanyahu, period. Netanyahu's actions on his recent visit (summer 2011) and treatment of the President of the United States were unforgivable. Republican members of the House of Representatives acted like pawns in receiving him with loud applause! This was disgraceful, politically based conduct. If a Republican President had received the same treatment, this conduct would never have occurred. The Israeli lobby in Washington, DC and the political contributions from Jewish sources in the United States obviously outweighed any concern for respect for the Office of President of the United States.

Obviously the pressure should be just as firmly and clearly put on the Palestinians to be reasonable and to think more about generations to come. Hamas and other terrorist groups have to be disbanded or neutralized in some realistic manner.

Israel under Netanyahu now threatens to attack Iran. The ramifications of this go it alone threat are incalculable. Netanyahu is a loose canon!

North Korea

North Korea is on one hand a complicated situation, and on the other hand, a simple situation with an uncomplicated solution.

We have begged, pleaded with and tried to buy North Korea's entry into the civilized world without success for too long. We need to advise China, Russia, Japan and South Korea that we are no longer going to lead or be a big player in negotiating with North Korea on any matter at any level. This is their part of the world, and it behooves them to deal with North Korea. Surely, they want a peaceful ,stable situation in their part of the world. They are climbing out of a 20th century that was not very constructive for their people, to say the least. They surely do not want to live another century under the threat of War, especially Nuclear War!!

We should simply advise that if North Korea makes any aggressive moves toward the United States, or our friends with whom we have mutual commitments to preserve peace and freedom, especially South Korea, we will take all necessary measures up to and including reducing North Korea to a dust bowl!

Make it clear that the United States does not want to be the big dog in the Far East. The United States just wants normal, peaceful relations with all nations.

The Chinese are an ancient, proud, brilliant people who have come a long way in the last half-century, and can be a very stable influence in this world. But, take heed that they are very smart, clever, tough negotiators and plan their moves well ahead and with great precision to reach their goals. They have completely outmaneuvered the United States in the past 30 years, especially in economic and business matters. They have used our big corporations and their capital, together with Chinese labor to out compete our national industries! They have used our greed against us. Our corporate CEOs, looking only to next year's bottom line, have moved large sums of capital and jobs into China, where their manufacturing costs are much lower. China does not want to accept being second to anyone!!

The United States has to get smarter and tougher in dealing with China. China understands and relishes the competitive game! The game does not bother them because they are confident in their ability to win more times than not. The United States has more marbles for the game, plenty of assets and smarts to compete.

Cuba

Our foreign policy re Cuba has been a total failure for over 60 years. The Cubans exiled by Castro and settled into south Florida have too long controlled the United States handling of relations with Cuba. Their blind refusal to accept reality has not accomplished anything positive for themselves or the Cuban people living under the communist regime of Castro. Why do we treat Cuba any different than China?

Chapter Ten

RIGHT TO BEAR ARMS

Why discuss the Second Amendment constitutional right to bear arms? It is a very important freedom to me personally and is, in my opinion, a very important freedom for every citizen of the United States whether or not a citizen chooses to own a firearm. Even though the United States Supreme Court has ruled in McDonald v Chicago that the Second Amendment to the Constitution applies to state and local governments, and guarantees the right of citizens to keep and bear arms for personal protection, the decision also clearly upheld the right of government (federal state and local) to enact reasonable gun-control laws. However, the court gave very little direction as to what gun-control laws can be enacted by state and local governments, except that a handgun can be kept in the home for personal protection. The court also acknowledged that laws preventing felons and the mentally ill from possessing guns and banning guns in sensitive places like schools and government buildings are reasonable and would not be in violation of the Second Amendment protection.

This decision was a five to four ruling. In my opinion, five to four decisions on major constitutional questions should not carry any weight. In this case, the dissenters expressed some very troubling approaches to an analysis of the Second Amendment. The majority left some big holes in their opinion as to the extent of the freedom of the people to keep and bear arms.

The Second Amendment provides:

> " A well regulated militia, being necessary to the security of a free state, the right of the people to keep and bear arms, shall not be infringed."

At the time the Constitution was written and adopted individual citizens were the "militia", a group with little structure at the Federal level, but in which every able-bodied male citizen was expected to serve in times of war, or other threats to the existence of the United States. Almost every adult male owned a musket.(long rifle)

The language of the Second Amendment does not have the precise clarity that those of us who support the right of every citizen to keep and bear arms for personal use would prefer. (e.g. hunting, sporting contests, recreation, and the personal protection of his or her person or property and other innocent human beings unjustly threatened with harm).

Those who would severely limit, and even totally deny, the right of citizens to keep and bear arms rely on this lack of clarity to push for greater restrictions on the right to bear arms.

They argue that the Second Amendment does not apply to deny states the right to infringe on (regulate or deny) the right of citizens to keep and bear arms because it only applied to the federal government when adopted. Further, they argue, it does not come under the" due process clause" of the 14th amendment, even though the 14TH Amendment has been held by the Supreme Court to also restrict the States from infringing on most of the protections of the first 10 Amendments.

This is a patently specious and untenable argument. Their analysis and arguments are not well taken. What good are the protections of the "Bill of Rights" (the first 10 amendments to the Constitution) if state governments can change, deny, regulate out of existence or otherwise avoid the protections of the Bill of Rights? Why the necessity of using the 14th amendment to apply the protections of the Bill of Rights to the citizen of the States in the first place? There is no distinction between citizens of the States and citizens of the United States!

The 14th Amendment, Section 1 makes it clear that the Bill of Rights does apply to the states. The privileges and immunities clause states: "no state shall make or enforce any law which shall abridge the privileges or immunities of citizens of the United States; ------".

Justice Scalia did not want to go this far in McDonald. Why not? I believe, because he obviously doesn't want that clear interpretation to apply to all provisions of the First, Fifth and Sixth amendments. Obviously he wants to be free to tweak the interpretation of women's right to choose cases and some criminal law cases involving the rights of criminal defendants.

Chicago's Mayor Daley's complaint that the ruling in McDonald would allow more guns in Chicago and, therefore, more gun crimes is patently not supported by history, or the facts. Criminals, obviously, have paid no attention to Chicago's anti-gun law and would not do so in the future. The enforcement of Chicago's anti-gun law left only law-abiding citizens without a firearm for personal protection. The same analysis applies to the District of Columbia's complaints after the Heller case was decided. The District Police Chief wanted regulations passed requiring all guns in the home, or other private areas, to be broken down, unloaded, and kept in a safe, making them useless for personal protection.

Opponents will also continue to cite the" militia" argument. Obviously, when our country was founded, almost every male in the country owned a gun or guns. The" militia" was armed citizens, not an organized military unit. The country was expanding West into unpopulated, large expanses. Any effort by any government entity or official to, in any manner, control guns or gun ownership would have caused another revolution! Hunting was a prime source of food even in the back country of the Eastern states. The protection of law enforcement officers was non existent or not effectively available.

There was at that time no question of the right to own and use guns. That unquestioned belief continued well into the 20th century. However, the need to have guns to hunt with for food decreased significantly with the growth of large urban populations. With that population shift, many households no longer possessed a gun.

Then came the post World War I "Gangster era" , the passage of the Prohibition Amendment to the Constitution and the development of automatic weapons, which were available to almost anyone. As a result, a serious law enforcement and public safety problem was created.

People naturally began to question the unfettered availability to anyone of automatic weapons with large bullet capacities, e.g. the " Tommy gun".

So began the debate re the Second Amendment protection of the right to bear arms.

The right to bear arms is, obviously, another freedom that has been constricted by the rapid growth of population and the concentration of population in urban/suburban areas. This change has lead to all kinds of social and economic problems which have resulted in the formation of gangs, the lack of a sense of community and the breakdown of local government control.

Dissents by Stevens, Ginsburg, Breyer and Sotomayor condensed the arguments, theories, and intellectual manipulations of the Second Amendment developed over the years since World War II to water down or totally destroy the Second Amendment right to bear arms.

Justice Stevens, in his own inimitable way, displayed and used his unquestioned intellectual talent and knowledge of the law to spin interpretations of the Second Amendment right of the people to keep and bear arms which would effectively give state and local government entities the power to severely restrict the peoples right to own and keep a firearm in a manner and in a condition to make it effectively available and usable for the protection of self, family and others.

Justice Breyer cited the loss of 60,000+/- lives a year from guns. He ignores the fact that a lot of human activity results in the death of human beings – e.g. driving motorized vehicles, using knives, ball bats, fire, hammers, etc. How many deaths will be prevented by restricting the right of law abiding, competent citizens to own, use or possess a gun? To restrict a citizens freedom, the benefit of doing so should clearly outweigh the loss of the freedom.

Most of the states have provisions in their constitutions which guarantee the right of citizens to keep and bear arms. Some mirror the U.S. Constitution Second Amendment. Most are clearer in their language than the Second Amendment as to the right of the people to keep and bear arms for the protection of person, family and property. West Virginia has the best and simplest. It includes hunting and recreation. Illinois is the worst. It provides: "subject only to the police power the right of the individual citizen to keep and bear arms shall not be infringed". That language is open to all kinds of judicial interpretation.

So the question is, in how much danger is the people's right to bear arms? The danger is significant even with the backup of state constitutions.

In my opinion, courts should simply find that, like a lot of other personal freedoms, speech, assembly, press, and use of property, the right to keep and bear arms can be reasonably restricted when it is necessary to protect the rights of other citizens (e.g. from slander, mobs, riots, yelling fire in a crowded public building). The Court should hold that the freedom to bear arms can be reasonably restricted when the benefit of the restriction clearly outweighs the loss of the freedom to bear arms.

Obviously, you cannot go down a street in a populated area (residential, business or otherwise) shooting a gun into the air or ground, or target practicing with a gun in your backyard in an urban/suburban setting.

Analysis of laws which show how this reasoning has not been used can be found in laws which deny a citizen the right to openly carry a gun (holstered or otherwise) anywhere in public, or openly carrying one in a vehicle, loaded or unloaded, The rights of other citizens are clearly not affected by citizens openly carrying or displaying guns. Some reasonable restrictions should apply and have been applied, e.g. age limits, no violent or felony criminal record or serious mental deficiencies or illnesses. However, law enforcement should be required to have probable cause to stop a citizen and interrogate based solely on the open possession of a gun. The same should be true with carrying a concealed weapon.

There was and is no necessity for hundred plus page court opinions to decide these issues.

Many gun owners, and myself also, resent the continued push by many anti- gun rights groups (and in many cases, by law enforcement) to restrict the sale of ordinary hunting guns by requiring the fingerprinting of purchasers and keeping records of the guns owned by citizens. Checking public records for felony convictions and serious mental problems should be sufficient. The records from such a search and purchase of a gun should be destroyed if the buyer's records are clean. No serial numbers should be kept by law enforcement.

Sales by individuals should not be regulated even at gun shows. The unnecessary restricting of the constitutional right to keep and bear arms by individual citizens far outweighs the potential threat to citizens that might be prevented by regulatory power in the hands of law enforcement agencies.

Law enforcement is already looking too much like a military unit in the design and decor of their uniforms and in performing too many of it's duties in too many communities across the country.

I have no use for the NRA! It's rigid approach to defending Second Amendment rights and the stupidity of its methods and programs, will in the long run, result in the anti-gun rights movement winning.

We need to make every gun owner and hunter an ambassador for the protection of the Second Amendment right to bear arms.

Wayne La Pierre ,President of the National Rifle Assoc., is either a person with little knowledge of the current makeup of society and the attitude of the majority of citizens toward gun ownership, (could care less or solidly opposes), or has undisclosed objectives. His recent attack on Pres. Obama was misleading, and without basis. He certainly turned me off and I'm sure he turned off a lot of other citizens and gun owners. My observations of Pres. Obama's Presidency is that gun control has never been and is not an issue which he has any desire to tackle.

The NRA's almost single-minded support of the Republican party turns off a major portion of the population, including a lot of citizens who support the Second Amendment right to bear arms. Its programs are too narrowly focused. The sad fact is, supporters of the Second Amendment right to bear arms are outnumbered by those millions who live in urban and suburban areas. A lot of those people care less about gun rights. They have a greater affinity with the avid gun control advocates who are gaining converts everyday. The battle will be won or lost depending on how well the supporters of the Second Amendment right to bear arms communicate with the urban/suburban citizens.

Positive programs about responsible gun ownership on television, the Internet and in other media will do a lot more good in the long run than supporting politicians with money. The political power in our government swings inevitably every 8 to 12 years.

The current Supreme Court has bigger fish to fry than spending too much of its public reputation and respect on the Second Amendment right to bear arms. Its makeup also changes regularly. I can just hear Scalia arguing his "original intent " theory to justify severe restrictions on an individual citizens right to bear arms in the configuration of semi-automatic weapons, even bolt action center or rim fire weapons, since ,obviously, such weapons were unheard of when the Constitution was written.

Mr. Ronald D. Schenck JD

Programs emphasizing the historic and positive place of guns in the hands of citizens during our democracy's growth over the centuries should be produced. Hunting is becoming a bad word. Emphasizing how hunters provide support for game habitat protection, enhancement and management, and how game herds and flocks have been restored by these programs will do a lot more to protect the right to bear arms than supporting politicians with money and other resources. The NRA"S totally unnecessary support of "stand your ground" laws is coming back to bite them hard and is clearly harmful to the protection of the right to bear arms.

The NRA should come out strongly against trophy hunting, ranch hunting and game farms, which are promoted for profit only. If you shoot it, you should have to dress it out, take care of the meat and eat it. If you cannot meet these requirements, then you simply should not be allowed to hunt. Hunting is not just going into the woods with a semiautomatic 7 mm Magnum, six shot, or more in a clip, and killing an animal, even if it takes six shots, or more and ruins almost all of the meat!

Further, it would be a good move for the hunting community, the NRA and other gun and hunting clubs to support a ban on using semiautomatic weapons to hunt with. Also, Magnums should be limited in their use to certain species in certain areas. You do not need a Magnum to kill a deer, elk, or black bear! I see no need for the regulation of ownership of specialty guns or semi automatic guns used in competition or recreational shooting at gun clubs or in open space remote areas.

I would accept a lot greater restriction on gun ownership rather than see the Citizens United case stand as law. Such a choice should not have to be made! Freedom in a complex and highly concentrated ,large population society, requires tough compromises.

If you carefully read Citizens United and MacDonald, you can, without much knowledge of the law, see that Citizens United is a much greater threat to all of our freedoms than MacDonald is a defender of the Second Amendment right to bear arms.

Citizens United is not only a total broadening of the meaning of free speech, it is in total contempt of how free speech has been defined by court precedent for centuries and is a total gift of almost absolute political power to corporations, unions and other powerful non political organizations and the very wealthy. Money in the control of entities created by law and used to control, or have effect on, the makeup and formation of the "peoples" government is free speech? Asinine! Corporations and other legal entities are "people"? ASININE! Read the First Amendment! Only human being citizens who speak singly or in groups re a common objective or belief are permitted to speak and engage in the political process of structuring or electing their government, and through law setting the rules by which they live.

It ought to be quite obvious that corporations, unions and the wealthy really do not care a whit about the people's right to bear arms!.

The long dissertation in Citizens United re attacking the validity of a "precedent" is clearly the establishment of a base to overturn any precedent decision which the majority does not like.

Justices Roberts, Alito, Scalia and Thomas are serious threats to many rights and freedoms long protected by "precedent". Justice Kennedy is not all that predictable, but reading Citizens United creates a lot of distrust of his judicial strength to stand up against the other four named above.

Citizens United threatens the very basis of our democracy. In the near future, the current Supreme Court majority would not shy away from severely limiting the right to bear arms to create the appearance of a balanced approach to mollify the critics on the left when they severely limit a woman's right to choose or expand government's support of religious schools or charities.

In the past conservatives have severely criticized the Supreme Court for a number of decisions made in the areas of free speech and the 4th 5th and 6th Amendments by what they considered a liberal court majority. I have agreed with them a lot of times. However, the decisions by the ultra conservative court majority in Bush v Gore and Citizens United go well beyond any "liberal" court decision interpreting the Constitution since the Great Depression. These decisions, in fact, make law-bad law and amend the Constitution by judicial fiat.

Chapter Eleven

THE CURRENT POLITICAL SCENE

The two-party system has failed in the many ways discussed herein and offers no clear program or vision which could have a realistic chance of getting this nation out of the gridlock our government is in, or first and foremost protecting our personal freedoms.

The Republican Party has been totally hijacked by rabid right wing bigots, racists, neo-cons, oligarchists and wealthy big business and investment interests who exhibit no responsibility or desire to support private or government sponsored social safety net programs, and especially no interest in paying their fair share of taxes to build and maintain the nation's infrastructure, of which they are the principal beneficiaries.

Neither do they exhibit any responsibility to support an education system which is key to providing them with people (our citizens) who can fill the jobs on all levels of their businesses.

The wealthy and big business's are thumbing their noses at lower and middle income citizens because they can take their money and other assets they have earned in the United States and invest abroad where taxes and the costs of doing business are much lower. Mitt Romney's Caymen Ils investments are a perfect example!!

Of course, they then lobby for no or little taxes on their profits when they bring them back to the United States and especially when they reinvest them abroad! Hiding their profits in Swiss Banks is also a popular avoidance scheme.

The economic collapse in 2007/2008 destroyed the Republican Party's chances of winning the 2008 election. Unemployment was rising like a tidal wave in 2008 and in 2009. Most of the job losses took place before Obama was sworn into office.

When Barrack Obama was elected President and took office in January 2009, the rabid bigots and racists among the ultra conservative free enterprise and right-wing air head Evangelical Christian Republicans , in their righteous wrath, found grounds to blame Obama and the Democrats for the economic collapse and unemployment. In early January 2009, these mindless bigots appeared as "the tea party" and blamed Pres. Obama and the Democrats for everything going back to the Great Depression! They appeared in Ku Klux Klan makeup and garb, and as old-time minstrel show caricatures and questioned Pres. Obama's birthplace and citizenship, and asserted that he was a Kenyan and not eligible to be President.

The tea party held rallies all over the U S and a number of Republican Congressmen joined them, and supported their ridiculous positions and charges.

President Obama and the Democratic majorities in the Congress were blamed for the national debt, the Wall Street bailout, the auto industry bailout and the continuing rise of unemployment. No matter that this all occurred, or was started, during the G. W. Bush years.

The cry of the tea party became "no more taxes, cut government spending" and do it by cutting every social safety net program. They called on every Republican member of Congress to oppose every piece of legislation proposed by the Democrats to get the country out of the deepening recession. These people had been nowhere in sight or sound when the Bush administration was creating huge deficits and getting into wars which were totally without basis or purpose. They ignored the fact that the Wall Street collapse and the mortgage fraud occurred during the GW Bush administration. They conveniently forgot the Bush tax cuts for the very wealthy, which added significantly to the budget deficits.

Sarah Palin, the defeated Republican vice presidential candidate, became the darling of the tea party. This, even though she had been exposed in the campaign to be totally incompetent to hold high public office. Palin was a stalwart, ultra right wing, religious conservative air head and she fit into the tea party perfectly.

The tea party membership, including a lot of Republican Congressman, made it clear that their primary cause was to defeat Pres. Obama and the Democrats in 2010 and kill Pres. O Bama's programs. Instead of proposing solutions to the recession, e.g. programs to reduce unemployment and home foreclosures, they just spewed hatred and all kinds of false factual claims re Pres. Obama's proposals: e.g. Obama is a socialist! Obama is not a natural born citizen of the United States! Obama is a Muslim! Obama is a Kenyan! When the public censure got too bad they cut out the racist signs and dress at their rallies.

They opposed Pres. Obama's "stimulus program.". When the stimulus program was over a year old they lied about the jobs it did create and the many more that it saved, especially in the area of public service e.g. teachers, police and firemen.

They opposed Pres. Obama's health care plan, and falsely charged it contained a death program for older terminally ill patients. They made other exaggerated criticisms as to its cost and its constitutional legitimacy. The moderate Republican members of the Congress obviously became so fearful of the tea party influence on their political base that they allowed the Republican Party to became a totally negative opposition party offering no positive alternatives or amendments.

The health care plan that was passed is a long way from perfect and does not come close to solving the long-term problem. The Republican minority, together with a few blue dog Democratic Senators and Representatives who profess to be "conservatives" and had, over the years, received strong support from the health insurance industry and other corporate lobbyists, killed any hope of developing an independent, nonprofit health care program run by private non profits.

The legislation that did pass required every citizen to purchase health insurance and provided financial help to lower income citizens to purchase health insurance.

The Republicans and tea party activists totally distorted this provision. They claimed it is unconstitutional. The Supreme Court will decide. So far, a majority of U S circuit courts have found it to be constitutional.

The stupidity of the attack on the health care act is revealed when it is analyzed in relation to history. Government has been involved in healthcare and its regulation for a century. Government got into providing health care with both feet with the passage of the Medicare and Medicaid programs in the President Johnson years. These programs did not raise any big scare about "socialism"! The providers of health care and their assets (hospitals, clinics, etc.) were not nationalized! Neither does the Obama/Democrat health care plan.

In addition, every taxpayer has been paying for the health care of those financially unable to pay since the Federal law was passed requiring hospitals, through their emergency care rooms, to provide healthcare to everyone who walks through their emergency room doors, even if they cannot pay! The emergency room law created a hidden tax which appears in every hospitals cost of doing business and is passed on to the public through higher fees and charges for health services rendered, or through higher taxes levied by the local healthcare districts. Government, in effect, nationalized the private hospital emergency rooms!!

The Republicans, including their tea party dimwits, never talk about this hidden tax, or in any way recognize its existence. Under their definition (which is not the historically recognized definition) this emergency room law is socialism! Why are they not against it and, in line with their concept of free enterprise health care, propose the repeal of the emergency room law the logical result of which would be a return to 19th century healthcare which lasted, in large part, into the mid-20th century. We could again rely on the " old country doctor's" and the charity hospitals to care for the indigent and lower income citizens. We could overlook, as we did back then, the many elderly who ended up being taken care of by their children, or were placed in miserable old people's group homes if they had no children able to take care of them.

Mothers to be could again give birth at home, with the care of mid wives or the old country doctor type, if they are lucky, as my mother did with nine of her sons!

If the Republican/tea party definition of " socialized medicine" prevents government from providing healthcare and we go back to a free enterprise, if you don't pay, you don't get healthcare system, then we can let our parents and grandparents die sitting by a window in a rocking chair (as my grandmothers did) having never had the benefit of an annual physical or any care for that growing tumor or other serious medical condition!.

The Republican/tea party, free enterprise above all philosophy, which protects the for-profit health insurance companies, should be held to explain the way they plan to avoid this result if they kill Medicare and Medicaid. Perhaps they would rather get rid of a few of the less privileged and worn-out old folks! God forbid, they do not even want to discuss end-of-life planning with the terminally ill.

I have never heard them explain what it is that private, "free enterprise" for-profit health insurance companies provide to better the delivery of healthcare that nonprofit, privately managed, government regulated healthcare providers cannot or would not provide. The cost of healthcare and health insurance is rapidly becoming impossible for our economy to bear.

These "free enterprise " at any cost, defenders have so totally misrepresented the problem and the issues to the American public that a majority support repeal of the Obama/Democrat health care law.

When the 2010 elections came along the tea party activists had sufficiently invaded the Republican Party to defeat some longtime moderate conservative Republican congressional members and to put forth candidates who supported their ultra right wing conservative programs. Republican members of Congress running for reelection, criticized the tea party at their own risk. Most of them embraced the tea party positions. The tea party's commitment to defeat President Obama and the Democrats was so fervent that they would have made a pact with the devil, if necessary.

The Democrats, Ah The Democrats!!

AH, The Democrats! They have let the Republicans and especially the tea party ultra right wing conservatives beat them with an unending loud din of bombastic falsehoods and half-truths. The Democratic leaders and Congressional members let the Republicans steam roll them in the 2010 election. So what is new! They tried to save their seats by pussyfooting.

Instead of taking a "give him hell, Harry" attitude and approach and defending the "stimulus program" and the healthcare law with a strong, loud and persistent recitation of the facts, they dodged and weaved and got their ass's kicked.

The Democratic Party is mostly impotent! Not incompetent, or dangerous, or living in the 19th century, like the Republicans, just no balls when it comes to a down and all out dirty political fight. They talk a good game but accomplish little. They have the ultra left wing component that believes every social/economic problem can be solved by another law or regulation, usually involving the creation of another bureaucracy. Just like the Republicans, Democrats also pander to big money if they want to be elected and re-elected. The current election cycle with Citizens United in effect is forcing them all into the big money Super Pac game.

Over the years since World War II and the "Great Depression" the two parties were not that far apart in their approach to governing. For the most part, everybody was rather fat and happy and nobody wanted to rock the boat too violently. Deals were made!

Democrats Truman, Kennedy, Johnson, and Clinton were all pragmatists – deal makers. Carter not so much.

Republicans Eisenhower, Nixon, Ford, Reagan and G.. H W. Bush were also deal makers. G. H. W. Bush got crucified for deal making re taxes!

However, especially over the years since World War II, the country has suffered greatly due to the parties inability to come together and face and solve economic and social problems looming as big as the midday sun and the results of this failure have come home to roost at the doorstep of both parties.

Some of them:

- Failure to meet our growing reliance on foreign oil when in the early 70s it hit us in the gut like a cannonball. It obviously was and is a serious threat to our economy and our freedom.
- Healthcare – Medicare and Medicaid and the failure to fund these programs by co-pays or additional payroll tax revenues or to pay for the add ons. Failure to recognize the rapid growth of the cost of healthcare and to develop practical programs to get control of that cost.
- Failure to put Social Security on a solid financial foundation for future generations.
- Failure to enforce our immigration laws and protect our borders.
- Failure to fund the maintenance of our infrastructure, including highways, bridges, airports, seaports, schools, and to fund and build new, innovative, transportation and electric power facilities.

- Failure to manage in any reasonable way the defense budget.
- Incompetent negotiation of free trade agreements.

The two-party system ,now with its total gridlock, has become the biggest threat to our Democracy and freedom of the individual citizen.

We need a new centrist party. Let the right wing "conservatives" have the Republican Party and the left wing "liberals" the Democratic Party.

The country badly needs a party that will focus on the freedom of the individual citizen of all income classes and recognizes that the opportunity and success of all classes depends on each class having a fair chance to succeed and no class having the power to control and own a disproportionate share of the financial wealth, capital, of the nation. We need a strong third-party that presents citizens for public office who are genuinely interested in meeting and solving our societal, economic and other problems with the highest goal being the protection of the freedom of the individual human being.

The Republican and Democratic parties have proven they are more interested in maintaining power than governing and providing solutions to social and economic problems. They, therefore, both pander to the big-money and other powerful groups. They cannot and will not change!

THE TWO PARTY SYSTEM MUST GO!!!

Chapter Twelve

THE COMING 2012 ELECTION

The country is set for another election fiasco. The Republican primary is already a down and dirty, big-money, no holds barred fight. The caliber of the candidates is depressing. None have stature. Are there any moderate Republicans in the Congress or State Governorships?

The Democrats appear to be going to operate in their normal totally inept manner. Their leadership in the Congress is pathetic. President Obama, a credit to the office of President, is saddled with the bigotry and racism that still exist, openly and covertly, in the population and amongst powerful segments of the political, economic and religious leadership in our great country.

President Obama is a great communicator, but a large portion of the population simply do not listen. Instead of an honest debate and constructive alternatives or modifications to proposed programs, there is arrogant, ignorant, bombastic diatribe. Then there are the outright bigoted, racist, mean little people who hate without mercy, but still claim to be good Christians! Especially the tea party radicals.

Then we have the Republican candidates for president who blame everything on Pres. Obama and the Democrats, totally forgetting the GW Bush administrations responsibility for the total economic mess we are in. What a pathetic group. Where are the Teddy Roosevelt's, Dwight Eisenhower's and Ronald Reagan's? Someone with stature? They all claim to be disciples of Reagan. They distort Reagan's philosophy and record and falsely assert beliefs and support for political, governing doctrines which he never expressed belief in or proposed, e.g., no new taxes ; no new programs unless paid for by cutting existing expenditures; programs to mix government and religion; giving non-political groups (corporations, unions.) unlimited financial power in choosing government representatives.

Mitt Romney, the nominee, has changed his beliefs and positions for or against almost every issue so that there is no way of knowing exactly what you're going to get in a President. He has cow-towed to, and attempted to please the ultra right wing conservative, religious evangelicals , and especially, the tea party. He is not a knowable quantity. Which Romney are you going to get? Certainly not strong leadership with the stature a President of the United States ought to have, no matter which one you get. Obviously he is a member of the 1% and talks that way.

Then there is Newt Gingrich! It is a disgrace that he was even in the race to be a candidate for President. It is discouraging and downright frightening that tens of thousands of people voted for him in the primaries. His record in public office is that of an unethical, egotistical, arrogant, self-serving political opportunist. His personal life has been and is a mess. He has demonstrated on a number of occasions that he is not a trustworthy person of integrity and honesty. He has been willing to do anything and take any position which he calculates will advance his power and make him wealthier! He has changed membership in religious denominations three times. The last time he left a Protestant church and joined the Catholic Church to please his new Catholic wife. Could he have demonstrated more clearly a total lack of a sincere and deeply held religious faith? At least Rick Santorum is straightforward in his religious beliefs and honest in them, as Middle Ages as they are!

Fortunately, a number of people in the loop in leadership positions in the Republican Party and in the conservative media spoke out against Gingrich's candidacy.

One can understand that those tea party members who are really just racists and bigots and have no regard for, care for, or understanding of true democratic government which protects the rights and freedoms of all citizens, vote for Gingrich, but it is of great concern when "evangelical" and other conservative Christian religious groups and denominations support and their members vote for a person of Gingrich's ilk!

Ron Paul distorts the meaning of " libertarian" as I have understood and used it over many years. He is certainly not a libertarian in the Goldwater tradition. Paul would shut down several government departments and a lot of programs and services now provided by government. If we could go back to one half or less of our current population and a simpler economy his governing model might be a reasonable position. Although he talks about freedom his "libertarian" philosophy no longer equates to greater freedom for individual citizens. Paul basically tows the current Republican Party line with the exception of his position against being the world's policeman and his isolationist foreign-policy. I agree that we should cease being the worlds policeman as I have explained elsewhere herein. However, his isolationist foreign policy is not realistic in the 21^{first} century.

Rick Santorum appears to be a decent, honest human being but he is a totally indoctrinated Catholic. His religious faith and philosophy predate Luther. He would continue and increase the co-mingling of religion and government. He proved to be too much of a right wing conservative for the people of Pennsylvania in his short service as a Senator.

All of the Republican candidates are accusing Obama and his administration of wanting to destroy all religious participation in our government. I have seen no evidence of that. The fact is, as it is now constituted, the Republican Party and the original group of Republican Presidential candidates present the greatest threat to religious freedom. People like Gov. Perry in Texas, Jim Diment from South Carolina, Michele Bachmann, Sarah Palin, John Boehner and the Tea Party bigots use and abuse religion at every opportunity. They use the threat that their opponents will , and have denied their children the right to pray in public schools etc ,as discussed herein re First Amendment rights. They are supported in this paranoia by the Evangelical, right wing, Christian church's . The mega church and TV ministries phenomenon that has sprung up in the last two decades and run by "ministers" who live the life of wealthy executives and support this political , religious scape-goating is the Elmer Gantry movement of the 21st century.

That great teacher, Jesus, would throw them out just like he threw the money changers out of the Temple. They are despicable representatives of the Christian religion. They sell religion like life insurance. The only problem is, at least with life insurance, your beneficiaries get the benefit. The biblical promise of heaven and life after death is free to every believer, all you really need is "faith", you do not need to pay for it! If it is there, and you believe, you will get it! Christ's teachings are available and free to all, as are the teachings of the prophets of all the great religious faiths. Christ's teaching was clear, do not mix religion and government.

Having been the principal cause of the greatest recession since the Great Depression, the Republicans now want to be returned to power, claiming that they can do a better job than Pres. Obama and the Democrats have done to try to clean up their mess. They obviously will use the same old Carl Rove tricks of fear, distortion and outright lies, re religion, homosexuality, etc. to win.

It would have taken an act of God to bring the nation out of the total economic breakdown which Pres. Obama inherited when he took office. With the tea party idiots nipping at their heels, the Republicans refused to engage in any constructive negotiations and opposed every program put forth by the Obama administration to pull the country out of this economic disaster. In the congressional elections of 2010 the Republicans used the same old tactics and gained a huge majority in the House of Representatives. In 2011, the Republicans unanimously opposed every program put forth by Pres. Obama and the Democrats to hasten the economic recovery. They proposed none, but they did push their ultra conservative, right wing agenda to deny women the right to control their own bodies! Almost nothing positive was accomplished by our government in 2011.

The Republican mantra was the tea parties mantra. They would not vote for anything except deep spending cuts in the social safety net and opposed any new taxes. The Republicans stuck with this position and the Republican presidential candidates supported it absolutely. This even though very few respected economists support this approach, liberal or conservative. Rather, most economists support a balanced approach with new taxes, and spending cuts together with government spending on much-needed infrastructure, both to repair and construct new, and on schools, as the best way to tackle unemployment and to get the economy rolling again.

Will the 99% of the electorate wake up, or will a majority of them be deceived again by Karl Rove tactics of fear, hate and the empty threat of losing their religious freedom.

Mr. Ronald D. Schenck JD

The country again faces the likely hood of a divided government and gridlock.

THE TWO PARTY SYSTEM HAS BECOME THE MOST SERIOUS THREAT TO OUR FREEDOM AND MUST BE ELIMINATED BY THE FORMATION OF A STRONG THIRD PARTY OR TWO !!!

Chapter Thirteen

THE OCCUPY MOVEMENT

The Occupy movement is an interesting and potentially positive political organizing force.

The question is, can they learn from the young people's movement of the 60s, which recognized that our society and political system had problems which were not being addressed by the people who controlled the power. However, they were not well organized, being made up of hippies, free love, rock music, anti-Vietnam War groups with little discipline. They totally failed to recognize and attack the problems with well thought out programs and changes in governing structure, which could effect real reform. Those 60s, young people are now the parents and grandparents of the "Occupy" movement members.

The problems in our political and societal system are much greater today. The Occupy movement, to be effective, must organize from the bottom up and develop clear objectives. Parades, Camp in's, and other forms of protest will not get anything accomplished. This is true especially when property damage and clashes with law enforcement occur.

They need to organize as a political party in every state. Financial support is critical. Identifying and pursuing the support of citizens and organizations with money and like concerns about the future of our democracy is also critical.

Identifying and recruiting candidates for congressional office in states and districts in which there is a reasonable chance of winning is the next very important step. Hopefully capable, reasonable, deliberative ,honest people who are interested in meaningful change can be found, as opposed to the tea party examples of ignorance, bigotry, racism , class warfare,and if you are not an Evangelical, born again Christian, you are going to hell, mentality.

The lower and middle income segment of our population has been deliberately and successfully attacked by the wealthy economic groups and individual citizens who in their selfish greed have figured out how to work the outmoded parts of our constitutional and political structure to gain and keep political power. Such disciples of this group as Boehner and McConnell blame the supporters of the middle and lower income citizens for pursuing "class warfare"! This, when the middle-class and lower income class have been losing economic position for at least 30 years and the wealthy class has prospered exponentially! Boehner cries at the threatened loss of the "free enterprise" economic system (his dreamed up fear). I have not seen or heard of him shedding a tear over the middle and lower income citizenry's loss of their homes or their being underwater on their mortgages. The personal freedom of the vast majority of our citizens has already suffered big losses and is threatened with even greater losses of freedom.

The Democratic Party has proven unable or unwilling to tackle this problem, some even support the Boehner view!!

No meaningful change will occur as long as the two party system controls the political power structure and thereby the government. To change this at least three objectives must be accomplished first:

1) Term limits for all elected government offices, local, state and federal. (See the discussion herein, Chapter Three)
2) the Supreme Court decision in Citizens United must be reversed or the First Amendment to the Constitution must be amended as discussed in Chapter Three..
3) the Constitution, 12th Amendment must be amended to eliminate the electoral college. (See the discussion in Chapter Three.)

This will require a long, committed struggle. This must be a commitment to our children, grandchildren, and on down the line.

My generation and the "Great Depression", WWII and Hippie/Vietnam generations have saddled the present generation of citizens under 30 with real problems that our generations have failed to address .A large percentage of our citizens ages 30 to 65 do not have a clue. They have lived the good life and inherited the financial largess created by their parents.

The Great Depression and World War II generation, The Greatest Generation , has good reason for the way they have lived their lives.The survivors of that generation came through some horrible years of deprivation and sacrifice. When World War II was over, all they wanted was peace and a decent living. They desperately wanted to provide a better life for their children. They could not fathom that the political system would end up in the shape it is in today. They built a strong economy and lived in the greatest country, and the greatest era of any ever experienced by a people on this earth. So has my generation. We need to recapture the dream.

We obviously did not transfer to our children and grandchildren the realization that sacrifice and eternal vigilance are necessary to gain and preserve freedom and the good life. Every generation is challenged. The challenges that come as a result of complacency and no big threats (e.g .no wars, depressions etc) are the most dangerous. Generations are created who believe they are entitled to the good life, and believe it will never end! In the pursuit of and defense of freedom, there is no rest. There are always those, who in their greed for more than they need will pursue their selfish agenda's without an iota of concern for anyone else or future generations. Greed is good! We have forgot that simple human weakness. There is no time for excuses or procrastination. Intelligent, deliberate strong and relentless action is required. The issues most dear to your heart and mind must wait until you control Congress and a majority of the State houses OR AT LEAST HAVE A VOTING BLOCK LARGE ENOUGH TO PARTNER WITH THE MEMBERS OF ANOTHER PARTY TO GET THE BASIC REFORMS DONE!

We still have the vote! Are you, this emerging generation, going to be conned out of using your vote to protect your generation and the personal freedom of future generations?

POST SCRIPT

We, the citizens of the United States, face the first major threat to our democracy and personal freedoms since the Civil War, and probably, the Revolutionary War!

The two-party political system is in a state of total stagnation and gridlock. The level of rancor, disrespect and outright vicious hatred between a lot of the Democrats , independents and Republicans, especially the tea party contingent, is frightening. Having observed the political scene for 60+ years and believing I had observed some very tough political battles, the recent era of campaigning and congressional infighting is so much worse than anything I had seen before that it makes it hard to believe that it is not a serious threat to our democracy. Even the current Republican primary has been totally without class, was degrading, even vicious.

What was our strong middle income class is now struggling just to survive. The lower and middle income citizens have little or no time or money to participate effectively in local, state or federal government. Many have turned for answers and comfort to religion, mostly ultra right wing conservative religious groups, e.g. Evangelicals. As in millenniums past, they become easy targets for manipulation and subjugation by clever, ruthless persons and groups who are without moral or ethical conscience and have no, or very little, sense of responsibility for any other human being or groups thereof. Our social contract is broken or does not exist. The strong take as much as they can get and control the rest. The rest survive as best they can under the thumb of the powerful.

The middle and lower income class have lost economic position in:
Income;
Home ownership;
Equity in their homes;
Ability to compete for jobs;
Availability and afford-ability of higher education.

The average entry wage level for high school graduates is over 20% below what it was in the 70s! The average entry wage for college graduates has only increased by a small percentage since the 70s!

The public school system is under constant attack from every quarter. Government investment in public school infrastructure, curriculum and staff has been declining for years.

Right wing, religious groups are succeeding in getting tax funds, which should be going to public schools, appropriated to their private schools. They cannot indoctrinate their children in public schools!

In the 20th century our public school system was a major contributor to the growth of our economic power. The public schools did not interfere with the religious schools or the private education of children of religious families!

The Republican Party has become the exclusive representative of the wealthy, powerful and religious conservatives. In the 2012 election primary they ran a one per center', a pre Luther, Catholic religious right wing conservative, a political prostitute and a take me back to the good old days "libertarian"! The Supreme Court's conservative majority is looking more and more like a pawn of the ultra-conservative wealthy, powerful, economic and religious groups, e.g. the Citizens United decision!

The radio waves are filled with the ultra-right wing conservative rants of the likes of Rush Limbaugh who are bought and paid for by the ultra-conservative, economically powerful people like the Koch brothers, who are poster boys for the passage of a high inheritance and gift tax.

Limbaugh should return to the cave from which he came and take Rove, Coulter, Beck, Ingram, Savage, Malkin and pretty boy Hannity with him. The problem is not the conservative Fox TV network. The problem is the citizens who listen and do not listen with a critical mind. For years citizens have complained about the "liberal media" (the major networks) and the "conservative media" (Fox network and talk radio, mostly). The problem is not with the media! The problem is with the close minded citizens who cannot listen to both and be able to sort out the wheat from the chaff. Rupert Murdoch, who owns a big share of, and runs Fox does not care a whit about the American democracy or freedom. Profit is his God! You just have to understand that! Citizens of all political persuasion must realize that all of the media, except PBS, are profit-based businesses. Most care about the professionalism of their journalists. Murdoch and Fox don't seem to give professional journalism much thought. If they did they would not hire people like Karl Rove, Beck, Ingram and North. I like Hemmer, Smith and Sustern. I watched O'Reilly for some time, until he finally wore me out with his frequent distortion of the facts and off-the-wall conclusions.

The major networks have also lost me for the most part. Controversy is not in their dictionary. Their reporting is pretty bland when it comes to the political scene and social issues, especially freedom on all levels! CNN does the best all-around job of balancing their reporting.

The Democrats are just ineffective.. Of course they have their bums to. They too are prisoners of the system and must rely on big-money interests to gain power and to keep it.

The independent voters and the youth of this new generation who are struggling to get a job, an education and a better life, need to wake up and organize a third political party to represent their interests and break the political gridlock.

If the current situation continues, the wealthy and powerful will rule in an oligarchy! Wealth will pass from generation to generation by inheritance.

T he 21st century will be a century of religious wars. Who will fight them? Not the wealthy! As opposed to the economic/social wars of the 20th century, I predicted in the early 1990s, that the 21st century would be a century of religious wars if we did not handle the rise of religious extremism very wisely and carefully. Then comes G. W. Bush and the neo-cons and the entry into wars with two Muslim countries for no good reason. Much better alternatives were available. We let a gang of criminal terrorists completely destroy our good judgment! We won the Cold War and an era of peace and prosperity beckoned and we blew it! Millions of Muslims think we hate them and want to destroy their religious beliefs. At this time in history, our brand of Democratic government, and probably any brand thereof, does not fit with the Muslim religion.

Can we get to a time when we no longer categorize one another as white, black, brown, or other; or as Muslims, Jews, Christians, or other; or as European, African, Asian, or other and just look at and describe one another as human beings, all searching for answers and no one having the final, the correct, or the absolute best answers. Can we find the ability and security to be tolerant, tolerant, tolerant of our multitude of differences?

IT'S A GOOD DREAM!!

It may be a dream, the fulfillment of which may be essential to our survival as a species!

I PROPOSE THE FORMATION OF A NEW POLITICAL PARTY NAMED "THE CONSTITUTIONAL FREEDOM PARTY".

CASE LAW CITATIONS

Case Law

    Citizens United v. Federal Election Comm. - 558 US 08-205 (2010)

    Witter v. Washington 474 US 481 (1986)

    Flast v. Cohen 392 US 83 (1968)

    Bowen v. Kendrick 474 US 481 (1988)

    Agostini v. Felton 520 US 203 (1997)

    Mitchell v. Helms 530 US 203 (1997)

    Zellman v. Simmons-Harris 536 US 639 (2002)

    Arizona Christian School Tuition Organization v. Winn

    US Supreme Court 09-987 & 991 562 F3d 1002 Rev.

    Trapp v. Dulles 356 US 86 (1958)

    Furman v. Georgia 408 US 238 (1972)

    Gregg v. Georgia 428 US 1531 (1976)

    McDonald v. Chicago 561 US 3025 (2010)

    Dist. Of Columbia v. Heller 554 US 570 (2008)

    Bush v. Gore 531 U S 98 (2000)

    Hosanna-Tabor Evangelical Lutheran Church v. EEOC 565 US___(2012)

INDEX

RESEARCH CITES

Lower and middle income classes-relative income compared to the wealthy income class:

    CNN Money-A Rough 10 Years for the Middle Class-5/16/2012
    USA Today.com -5/16/2012
    Mother Jones-Only Little People Pay Taxes-3/18/2012

Federal Estate and Gift Tax Law:

    Findlaw
    Answers.Com

Gross National Debt-Clinton to G. W..Bush to Obama/ 2000 to present:

    Office of Management and Budget
    Congressional Budget Office
    Wikipedia

Unemployment-2000 to present:

    Bureau of Labor Statistics
    Workforce Explorer
    Wikipedia

Economists and - Cutting Taxes Or Stimulus:

    Pew Research Center - Debt and Deficit
    Yahoo News-10/30/11/ GOP Candidates Plans

CPSIA information can be obtained at www.ICGtesting.com
Printed in the USA
LVOW131902180912

299318LV00028B/325/P